About the author

Carrie Jones is the pseudonym of a successful publishing executive. *Cutting Up Playgirl* is her first book.

CUTTING UP PLAYGIRL

CUTTING UP PLAYGIRL

A MEMOIR

Carrie Jones

First published in Great Britain in 2008 by Old Street Publishing Ltd

This edition published 2009 by Old Street Publishing Ltd
28–32 Bowling Green Lane, London EC1R 0BJ
www.oldstreetpublishing.co.uk

ISBN 978 1 905847 61 7

Copyright © Carrie Jones 2008

The right of Carrie Jones to be identified as the author of this work has been asserted by her in accordance with the Copyright, Designs and Patents Act 1988.

All rights reserved. No part of this publication may be reproduced, stored in or introduced into a retrieval system, or transmitted, in any form, or by any means (electronic, mechanical, photocopying, recording or otherwise) without the prior written permission of the publisher.

10 9 8 7 6 5 4 3 2 1

A CIP catalogue record for this title is available from the British Library.

Printed and bound in Great Britain

	Introduction	1
1	Still Life	7
2	Jerky Boys	19
3	Stories of *Ow*	33
4	Awfully Hot	49
5	Kissing Caroline	55
6	Fascist Regime	67
7	*Allons, enfants de la patrie*	76
8	Losing It	96
9	Cold Fish	116
10	No Paris Hilton	133
11	Twitching in Cambridge	140
12	Rome Express	151
13	Italian Meatballs	163
14	Extra-Marital	176
15	Magic Journey	194
16	Mark as Read	208
17	All the Things I'm Scared of	228

Twenty-three men.

There are three whose surnames I can't remember, including one whose name eludes me entirely.

Ten were proper boyfriends.

I slept with nine of them only once: five of those were people I already had crushes on, one was dressed as a woman.

One was Korean-American, one was Italian.

One was Jewish.

Two were married.

Two were brothers.

One gave me scabies.

Two were significantly older than me.

One of them was 'good in bed', two of them were terrible in bed and two felt faint after sex.

One had to have the radio on all night and one kept up a tormenting monologue during sex.

There are five that I came to dislike intensely, three that I would sleep with again if I had the chance. I really regretted having sex with six of them.

One had an unusually large penis and two had unusually small ones.

None of them 'gave' me an orgasm, except one – possibly. I wanted it to happen so badly I think I believed my own faking.

One is now dead.

I loved three of them.

I was engaged to three of them (not the same three) and married one of them.

Of course, the men I didn't get to sleep with are just as important.

INTRODUCTION

MY sexual desire started digging its way underground long before I had any actual sexual experiences. As a child, an instinctive feeling of shame (about almost *everything*, I'm ashamed to say) gave rise to a great secretiveness – my strategy for dealing with the embarrassment that constantly engulfed me. If nobody knew what I was doing, or thinking, then I could act and think with impunity. There would be no need to worry about what anybody – especially my mum and dad – thought of me. My parents were, to all appearances, perfectly tolerant: they never told me what I could and couldn't do, they were never angry, they never tried to tell me that sex was wrong. No, but perhaps that's because I had absorbed their unspoken taboos at such an early age, and been so successfully transformed into an obedient and unchallenging daughter, that there was no need for them to keep on ramming the message home.

When a toddler, I once ran out into the traffic without warning and gave my mother a terrible fright. In her alarm she walloped me hard, a moment of uncontrollable rage, perhaps, that I had tried to escape from her. From then on, I never again threatened to leave the magic casing she had thrown up around the two of us until I got married, quite late in life – and even then it was more that the casing gradually grew thin and wore away rather than that it was torn down. Until then, she and I were as one, an undivided mind.

A mother and her child are merged when the child is first born, and that's natural, the way it needs to be. But usually the child separates from the mother, in stages, gradually becoming their own person. Of course the separation causes anxiety on both sides but if the mother is sufficiently strong in her own sense of self, then she will let the child emerge without feeling too great a sense of loss. In my mother's case, I believe she thought having a baby would be completely magical and that the baby would overwhelm her with love, filling the gap left by her own less than loving mother. The discovery that a baby is endlessly needy and that she was expected to fulfil those needs – rather than the other way round – must have been a profound psychological shock.

Once the first two years of dependence were over, though, it became possible to skew the deal the other way, to start to claim something in return for all that had been paid out. If that happens, then in effect the child becomes servant to the parent, fulfilling the mother's fantasy of having a 'beautiful little girl', an accessory that makes the mother look good, always there to listen, sharing secrets. This is what happened to me – I was inside my mother's bubble and, knowing no other way, I was happy in there, pleasing her, privy to all her secrets, laughing about people with her, ganging up against my dad. I had absolutely no sense that this might not be the best way to be, and did nothing to undermine the way things were between us. The punishments that might be brought to bear on me if I did… well, who knew what they might consist of? Some form of annihilation?

However, even within the bubble, it was still possible to hide things – thoughts, words, desires – and so to keep oneself alive and in some sense separate, even whilst reassuring my mother that nothing was changing.

But any overtly 'sexual' things I did were, firstly, delayed long after the age when most adolescents start to take an interest in sex and, secondly, constrained by what I felt my parents would be able to bear. The things that really excited me were already stored safely away. So whilst the *idea* I had of sex (which had evolved through my secret readings of the books in the special drawer upstairs and of my dad's soft-porn magazines) was dark and explicit, the reality was incredibly tame. Anything that threatened to make my pulse race had to be hidden from sight.

Why would somebody with such a veiled sexual life suddenly decide to reveal all? What if people should read it and *find out*? I think I must be experiencing a grotesquely delayed adolescence – it was basically this or tattoos and body-piercing. The teen rebellion is finally happening, it's just that I'm forty-three. But, undeniably, it is also the result of sublimation: my thwarted desire has found an outlet in these pages.

I've felt myself driven by sexual steam-power before – it usually takes the form of embarrassingly juvenile 'grand projects'. A boyfriend to whom I was engaged but for whom my feelings had completely died must have been bewildered when I undertook to recreate the Mexican Day of the Dead in the spare bedroom of our flat in Crouch End.

For months I sat in our small kitchen funnelling my deadened sexual energy into making papier mâché skulls, dancing cardboard skeletons and crêpe-paper marigolds. Then, as All Souls Day drew near, I made 'shrines' in the spare room, heaping exotic fruit and bottles of pale Mexican beer in front of blown-up photographs of my great-grandfather (a very bluff Yorkshireman, and almost certainly not a fan of fancy fruit and weak foreign beer) and his daughter, my granny. Enough fairylights and candles to pose a quite serious fire hazard, what with all the doilies I'd used as edging, and the effect was almost complete. On the Night of the Dead itself, I put on a tape of teeth-jarring mariachi music and scattered rose-petal confetti from the front door of the flat to the pink spare-bedroom carpet – in Mexico real flower petals lead in the souls of dead ancestors to indulge in the treats the family has laid out for them. As well as the poor boyfriend, who had to live with this madness, I had invited all my friends to enjoy the spectacle I'd prepared for them over so many weeks. As they arrived, I began to sense a collective reluctance to enter the spare room. Perhaps it was the tang of incense that disturbed them, perhaps the jangling guitars of the mariachi band were not to their liking. Maybe the voodoo Catholicism of the festival unnerved them. Of course it was only *pseudo voodoo*, in this case, but soon they were all huddled in the kitchen, taking comfort in the chilli con carne and avoiding talking to me. In my Day of the Dead shrine in the bedroom, the candles burnt low and one of the frilly trifle cases they were standing in started to smoulder. My great-grandfather, stern in his tinsmith's overall and strangely warped because I'd photocopied him from a very old, bent photo, looked offended by this exploitation of his memory. As a social event, the night was a disaster. No one would touch the exotic fruit, and when I brought out a bottle of tequila, first one and then all of my guests made hasty excuses to leave.

Not too long afterwards, I managed to tell the boyfriend it was over and my sexual energies soon had new and more conventional channels through which to sluice. So perhaps, by comparison, a book is not too outlandish a product of sexual frustration.

I can't lay claim to any great trauma that might colour my narrative with gothic: no fashionably horrific abuse (unless you count the hairy knitted matinee trousers I always had to wear to the cinema as a small child), no serious neglect, no eating disorders, no drug addictions, no direct encounters with death as yet. My existence surely falls within the bounds of what's termed 'normal'. In fact I think many aspects of my personality are signs of a protracted 'childhood'. Like a child I hate strong alcohol, cigarettes are even 'yukkier', drugs just scary; high heels and make-up are something to play dressing-up in occasionally but feel ridiculous. Being a 'sensible girl' is second nature to me.

As for my wicked 'inner sexpot', you have to wonder how much reality she can have if she hardly ever gets an outing. How long can she sustain me with her promise of erotic fulfilment if she is never integrated with my other persona, the School Librarian? When I re-read the endless letters I wrote to my mother (from childhood to well into my thirties) I'm nauseated by the false tone of them, the sugary cooings of adoration, the safe chitchat about art exhibitions and craft projects. Worse still, my childhood and teenage diary entries are the same, as if I feared that they would be read by my parents and so must keep up the same loathsome sweetness. I want to revisit my past and write an account of it to show that there was something else going on in my head beyond the 'super walks' I went on and the 'delicious goodies' I ate, the jigsaws and choir practices. For every phoney page in my diary, there was another reality in which a girl who had found out secret stuff about the power of the sexual drive, and who was both afraid of it and fascinated by it, tried to hide her knowledge, her knowingness from those closest to her.

Picking my way through the dot-to-dot of my sexual experiences may show up some of the reasons why I have ended up, in my early forties, split into two mutually hostile sexual personae: one withdrawn, rebarbative, sour, the other driven, curious, prepared to take risks – Mary Whitehouse arm-wrestling with Emma Bovary. I have a feeling, a fear more like, that the married woman who has put an end to sex is intimately connected to the would-be adulterer who harvests sweetness from every encouraging look, every flirtatious encounter, who devours sexual images and words and longs to make them flesh. An efficient way to over-sexualise everything is to banish sex itself, normal, boring, if-it's-Saturday-it-must-be-sex sex. Then all that's left is the promise of sex, fantasy sex, and you don't even have to get your hands dirty.

Chapter 1

STILL LIFE

They had packed all their movable furniture into the van, wrapped all their ornaments in muslin and left dear Swallowcroft...

Dr and Mrs Marsh travelled up to Cambridge by second class train but Hilary had to go with the furniture on the cart... The cart stopped abruptly outside a small whitewashed cottage... Hilary burst through the door and stood panting.

'Mama!'. 'Papa!' she called, but there was no answer. Suddenly Hilary felt an icy wind against her face. She noticed how cold and unwelcoming the dusty cobwebs looked and how bare the rotting wallpaper looked. Hilary realised that she was alone... Not only was there the prospect of spending a night alone in this grim dark house but the thought of her mother and father travelling on a train through the dusky evening. Then she had a terrible thought: what if her mother and father had been in a crash?... She walked slowly up the twisting path. She did not notice how beautiful the mellow sun looked through the amber leaves as it set, nor how the gentle breeze rippled the pond into a distorting mirror. Hilary was Alone.

Extract from 'Hilary's Story', completed 16 January 1974 (age 11)

WHEN I was ten, in the summer between leaving primary school and starting at the local comprehensive, we moved house. We left the two-up-two-down cottage that my parents had rented off my maternal grandmother to move into a much larger house that they had bought at auction. It was a big Victorian terrace on one of the main roads out of the town ('main road' being a relative term – it still had pavements raised above the road to make it easier to get in and out of your carriage). There would have been a wonderful view over the whole valley if it hadn't been for the equally big houses over the road obscuring the view. My mother had spent a great deal of her childhood and youth in the enormous red-brick house almost opposite, which had belonged to her granny and grandfather. It was to that house, in the early Fifties, that she had brought her glamorous new acting friends back from rehearsals at the local theatre. And where they had heard great-grandfather peeing loudly into a tin bucket (which he had made himself) in his room next to the kitchen while they were drinking instant coffee and attempting to chat vogueishly.

When I first saw inside the new house it had just been vacated by tenants and was still crudely divided into two flats. A chunk had been sawn out of the banister rail which curved up all three floors to accommodate a cheap plywood door at the top of the first flight of stairs, and all the rooms beyond this door were the domain of the upstairs flat. The upstairs tenants would have had to come in and out of the house through the downstairs people's territory so there must have been awkwardness. The downstairs flat had only half as many rooms as the upstairs one, but they included the grand front drawing room by way of compensation.

I remember that first visit and the seemingly endless floors stretching up and up. It was huge compared to our cottage, but it was also cold and dirty and unlovely. The back part of the house felt as though it was tacked on, although in fact it was part of the original building. There were three rooms sandwiched into the ground floor of this back part: the kitchen, a bathroom (which was a narrow slice stolen from the kitchen, put in as a grudging necessity when the house became flats) and the 'Orange Room'.

Today, over thirty years later, this living room is still known as the Orange Room, for when we first saw it that day it was entirely painted with thick gloss paint in a neon shade of orange. Even the light switches and cupboard doors were orange. As soon as we moved in, my father covered the ceiling in polystyrene tiles and the walls in anaglypta as a matter of urgency, but the room remained orange in memory.

My father worked very hard all that summer to make the house habitable for us. For the move itself he borrowed a pick-up truck and he and my uncle loaded it with our furniture, which wasn't much. I was allowed to ride in the back of the truck for the short journey through town. This was unprecedented and also frightening: jolloping along the cobbles reminded me of the time when the door of my dad's car had accidentally come open next to me as we went over the cobbles and, terrified, I had seen them rushing along beneath us. Whenever I see *The Grapes of Wrath* it reminds me of that brief trip as an Okie, which I now think my father may have deliberately set up in order to embarrass my mother. She wasn't involved in the move because, as a town councillor, she was required that morning to take part in a solemn procession of dignitaries through the town to the Parish Church. It was surely not a coincidence that the beat-up truck, piled high with our humble belongings and with a grubby child perched on the tailgate, should lurch through town just as my mother was slow-stepping through the marketplace in her best outfit. I'm sure he honked the horn and waved.

Once we were in, there was a territorial battle between my parents over who should choose the decorative style of the rooms. It being the early Seventies, both of them had strong ideas about décor. My mother had been heavily influenced by Terence Conran's Habitat and by Laura Ashley. My father disliked Mum's ideas on principle. She managed to grab control of the core rooms while conceding the downstairs bathroom, the top-floor bedrooms and what had been the kitchen of the upstairs flat. This last room became his 'workshop' where he would spend increasing amounts of time.

In the downstairs bathroom, the black enamel paint favoured by my dad in all practical tasks was dominant. The floor, the tiled splashbacks, the panelled sides of the bathtub – all were soon painted the glistening black of wet tarmac. Inspired by one of his favourite artists, 'Douanier' Rousseau, he papered the walls with a dense stylised jungle print. If my dad had embraced the 'crazy' Sixties to any greater extent than wearing black polonecks and having a copy of the Penguin Liverpool Poets in the loo, it might have had been suspected that he had decorated this room whilst under the effect of psychedelic drugs. There was no heating in this bathroom and steam never cleared from its clammy confines, so, as a precaution, he carefully varnished the wallpaper with high-gloss polyurethane. The added gleam completed the impression of being pressed in upon by giant succulents, where acid-crazed monkeys might descend from the mist-tendrilled trees at any moment and tear out your eyes as you peed.

My father also got to decorate the upstairs loo, which he chose to do with a highly fashionable collage of women cut from the pages of the *Sunday Times* colour supplement. This trumped what his bachelor friend had done, which was to hang a board on the back of the loo door pasted with a melange of women's bodies and faces. The friend taught in a convent school and could not risk the opprobrium of the Mother Superior if she should call on him at home and need to use the lavatory. In case of such visits, the board was turned round to show a portrait of the Queen on the other side. Our family, apparently, had no such concerns, and so the back wall of our loo, carefully shaped around the cistern, was entirely papered with heavily made-up eyes, scarlet lips, breasts, Modigliani nudes, Brigitte Bardot and other starlets, Picasso's *Les Demoiselles d'Avignon* (which I've always hated) and countless other fragmented women. I don't know if they were intended to provide any sort of stimulus, but the pictures were behind you if you sat down, so not easy to contemplate from that position. Nonetheless, I was very aware of them. There was a particular grouping of eyes, nose and mouth – three separate cutouts – up on the left which, together, made a grotesque face and I always tried to avoid making eye contact with that Gorgon as I feared it would put the evil eye on me.

It wasn't long before the new house had absorbed us. We soon established arrangements for living there which then continued for years, never varying until I had left home, and even beyond that, until my parents got divorced. Those years of routine – those meals cooked and eaten, those cups of tea in bed, those baths where you huddled beneath the taps to keep the last gallon of warm water around your knees after all the water behind you had gone grey and cold – are impossible to differentiate. They stand as a solid block, seven years long for me, during which our habits created battlements which must not be stormed. These routines were the very infrastructure of our privacy as a family, and it went without saying that, like the Borrowers, we did not want to be *seen* living the way we did. It wasn't that it was *so* shameful, but our routines would have been disrupted by visitors and that in itself meant casual visitors were to be discouraged. There was a strong sense of reliance on the sameness of things, on familiarity and predictability, to anaesthetise the pain of unhappiness. The unhappiness itself was utterly routine.

My father put a Parkray fire into the Orange Room and, the only reliably warm place in the house, it became the nest room. The butter dish always sat on the slate mantelpiece above the fire to soften the butter, which as a result was always slightly rancid. The damp salt, a coppery blue-green, was also kept there.

My mother and father got dressed down in the Orange Room every morning – separately, of course – stooping to step into their underwear in front of the Parkray. Mum kept most of her clothes in the bottom of the large cupboard to the left of the fire, and dad kept his in the corresponding cupboard on the right. These were huge cavities, floor to ceiling. Mum kept her underwear stuffed in the drawers of the dresser, which also contained piles of magazines, bills and bank statements, medicines, the striped box with her hairpiece from the Sixties, art materials, and the very many zippered bags and old chocolate boxes containing her make-up.

Only once in all the years of my parents getting dressed in front of the Parkray did I see something I shouldn't. I was used to seeing my mother naked – she never locked the bathroom door and thought nothing of summoning me to talk to her there – but my father's body was very much taboo. So much so that I knew nothing of his dressing rituals, always coming downstairs to find his ancient towelling dressing-gown hanging on the back of his cupboard door; this proved that he had come downstairs in it, although he was always fully dressed by then. The dressing-gown was unpleasantly short, and showed not only his hard white calves (threaded with veins that made me think of Blue Stilton) but also his knees, which were like twin pots of face cream, their surfaces smooth but uneven. Only once did I come in through the door without pausing and see him at the very moment of maximum stooping, his back to me, one foot already hooped by the leghole of his Y-fronts, something dark and pendulous dipping down beneath the worn hem of the dressing-gown. After that I learnt to look through the heavily ribbed square of glass that was set into the door before going in. The ribs sheared the view of the room into disguising slices but it was possible, nonetheless, to discern the dark-green dressing-gowned form of my father if he was not yet dressed – in which case I would turn aside to the cupboard under the stairs and crouch there to sort out the books I'd need for the day's lessons or perhaps polish my shoes. It was hardly ever necessary to do this, in any case: minute adjustments – him carefully starting to dress a little earlier, me carefully taking a little longer to clean my teeth – meant that he was usually sitting rolling his cigarettes for the drive to work by the time I opened the Orange Room door.

The Orange Room was a dressing room, then, but it was also the room where things were supposed to dry. The collapsible wooden dryer was nearly always up and hung with damp clothes which dried stiff and grey. Mum wasn't interested in white goods. She hadn't woken up to spin cycles and tumble drying and fabric conditioner (and in fact never would). It was not so many years since I had helped her feed the handwashed clothes through the mangle in the back yard of our old house. *A mangle!* When we moved to the big new house, a washing machine was bought, a huge step forward into a technological world of wonder. But the machine that Mum chose was already almost obsolete for she picked out the contraption which most closely mimicked, mechanically, the ancient copper of her childhood. This washing machine had to be filled by hand with buckets of hot water. Then, on shutting the lid, a churning motion began which drubbed the clothes for as long as one wished. Then you had to fish the sodden, soapy bundles out of the machine's narrow chamber, rinse them by hand, and, having meanwhile emptied the dirty water out using the rubber hose at the back, slap them back in for spinning. The machine actually made doing the laundry more laborious, not less, and was a poke in the eye for modern Britain. The clothes and sheets came out of the spin moulded into fantastic cones and coils, the creases so fiercely embedded into the fabric that no amount of ironing could remove them, especially after they'd been fixed like papier mâché by the Parkray. The final step was not so much to fold the washing as to *bend* the items at various hinge-points until the pile waiting to be taken upstairs resembled sheets of medieval vellum.

Sometimes my dad took the laundering of his clothes into his own hands. In order to preserve the proper division of labour by gender, it was necessary that his way of doing his 'dhobi' was entirely different from my mother's and very male (akin to a man only deigning to cook if it's on a barbecue). He would occasionally boil an armful of underpants in the large brown enamel pan that was otherwise only used on those rare, not to say aberrant occasions when Mum tried to make strawberry jam. Who knew why the underwear must suddenly be boiled, but I sensed that the ceremony represented a release of frustration following an inexorable build-up of dissatisfaction with the cleanliness of his undergarments. I imagined there must be some quality of the fabric, a mustiness, or a fine dust clogging the cotton fibres, which eventually became intolerable and must be attacked in an aggressive male way, rather than by Mum's patently ineffectual methods. It was literally a letting-off of steam, and as he prodded at the bubbling cloth with the handle of a wooden spoon (as if this were somehow more hygienic than using the other end) grey vapour billowed around his head like a genie. It was impossible to say whether he was happy or angry to be boiling his knickers; he seemed to have the gift of being both simultaneously. Mum hated him doing this, which of course gave it a pleasurable edge: he was righteous in his commandeering of the stove because it was *her* failings as a laundress which forced him to take this drastic action.

The one thing we didn't do in the Orange Room, which we might have been expected to do since it had a huge table in it and was right next to the kitchen, was eat our meals. Apart from Sunday lunch, we always ate in the telly room. The routines associated with this room were even more sacred than those of the Orange Room and there was a strong sense of its being a sanctum. The telly room was always in shadow, trapped in the armpit of the L-shaped house, and the walls were higher than they were wide, which gave it the feeling of an ancient bailey. The thickly gathered net curtains at the window shut out still more light. Sometimes the boy with long hair in the house across the back alley would hang out of his bedroom window for hours on end and then it was good to have the nylon nets obscuring the view.

For all the years that I lived in that house, I would come home from school and sit on the little foot stool in front of the Gas Miser watching children's television. The fire always had to be on because it could be the hottest day of the year outside, the heat would never come inside. The side of one leg would become mottled by the heat, while the rest of me remained cold. The little stool was my place, between my mother's brown corduroy chair from Habitat and Dad's wide, low chair with flat squares of wood at the ends of the arms, imprinted with rings of dried coffee. Squatting on the stool, my knees came up towards my chin and my school skirt slipped down into folds around the top of my legs.

Cutting Up Playgirl

Underneath the chinkling music of *Wacky Races* or *The Singing Ringing Tree*, whatever was on, I would hear Dad reversing the car into the garage at the top of our long, narrow back garden. Could I *actually* hear it, or did I just sense it? The revving engine thickened the air with its vibrations and the skin on the back of my hands responded by tingling. He always sounded angry backing in.

I would hear the garage door slamming shut, the bit of nailed-on plank at the bottom scraping on the cracked concrete because the hinges had dropped. Then the ting of the latch on the gate going up, the gate clinking shut, and his feet striking down the path. He always walked down the path in the same way, as though he hoped sparks would fly from his soles.

When he came into the room I smelled him straight away. The grey leather car coat and the cigarettes. It was only when I was older that he took to keeping the coat on when he came in. The leather was thick and rode up around his neck when he sat down in his chair. He looked uncomfortable, as if he was on the verge of leaving at any minute, and I think that was the point – he wanted to believe that his continuing to stay in the house was provisional, that he was free to leave. And so he was, though it took him decades to do it.

'Now then.' His voice always sounded slightly projected when he said this, the vowels tightened. He'd been trying to lose his north-east accent for years.

I would pull my skirt down over my knees and wrap my arms round them.

'Let's have a sight of the fire, then.'

Reluctantly I would push my heels into the carpet and the stool would move back a foot or so. The heat of the gas fire no longer reached me. There was that thickening feeling in the air again; he wanted to talk to me, but the things he said were usually wrong.

As the news headlines began, my mother would push open the telly room door with the edge of the tea tray and put the tray down in front of the fire. Having been brought down the unheated passage from the back of the house, the food was never very hot.

My father's face would register sudden pain, a trapped nerve perhaps, or a stab of toothache.

'Did you warm these plates?'

Mum's eyes would swivel towards me and cross very slightly.

If my dad had a further problem with the food he would do the *papping* thing, churning a suspect mouthful between his tongue and the roof of his mouth. Of course he wanted Mum to ask him what was wrong with the food, but she wouldn't. She listened intently to the news.

Dad would then elaborately spit the mouthful of offending food, say runner beans, onto his plate, not at the side but on the highest peak of his mashed potato.

'Stringy tasteless things.'

He would put the plate down on the floor, lever himself up out of his armchair and go out, leaving the door open.

Mum would hope he wasn't coming back so that she could put *Crossroads* on. Dad could not tolerate *Crossroads*. But then the door would open and he'd come back in again with a doorstep of bread and jam. Sighing, he'd sit down heavily in the armchair again, still in the coat, which was like a statement of his unhappiness.

Then Mum might do the thing with her tongue, sticking the tiniest tip of it out of the side of her mouth and waggling it at Dad, while her eyes stayed innocently fixed on the telly. I would see it and be complicit in the mockery. That was how we got one back at him when he was in a state. One of the ways.

After a few minutes, Mum might nudge my thigh with her foot and then, when I looked up, signal towards Dad with her eyes. He'd be asleep, the tea plate in his lap and crumbs skiing down the grey slopes of the coat, his lips pressed sourly together.

'Put *Crossy* on.'

I'd creep forwards on my hands and knees towards the telly. First you had to turn the volume down, slowly, imperceptibly. Then with one hand waiting to cushion the BBC1 button as it popped back up, gently press the Tyne Tees button down. The sharp retorts of the buttons could easily wake him, but if we were lucky we'd get to see almost all the day's excitement at the Brummie motel. If my dad woke up and discovered it was on, he would immediately walk out and go up to his workshop. After he had gone I would feel guilty and hollow, the pleasure of watching the forbidden programme vanished.

This is how it was for years, until I started to change. Then there came a threat that incomers – *boys* – would try to storm the citadel and upset the morbid equilibrium.

Chapter 2

JERKY BOYS

I went up in the library with Mark. We were reading and talking about things (music, the French Communist Party, the Fool in King Lear*). Then he was reading me poems and I didn't want to go home at all except that he remembered he had to go home to go to Manchester for his sister's wedding.*

Diary entry for February 15th 1979 (age 16)

MARK Sykes was a boy who seemed like a man, even in school uniform. He came into our sixth form from another school, he had the glamour of the unknown; we hadn't seen him grow up, heard his voice drop, seen the first whisper of stubble on his chin. He appeared fully formed, apparently mature. My attraction to him was so strong that it shut off all the usual outlets that would normally compensate, in part, for the frustration of longing to go out with someone. I liked him so much that I kept my liking to myself — no sharing him with my best friend, no special dropping of his name, loaded with nonchalant significance, into break-time conversation. He was The One.

He was tall enough, and he wore the black school uniform like a business suit. His hair had a shape, where all the other boys either had scrubby crops or unkempt messes (which secretly they imagined gave them rock-star profiles — Emerson, Lake and Palmer were gods among the boys at my school). His face seemed wonderfully serious, as if he were contemplating Important Things, such as the meaning of Rimbaud's poetry or how to get to Newcastle for a New York Dolls gig. While Mark's best friend Neville grimaced and guffawed like any seventeen-year-old boy, Mark was self-contained, enigmatic. I adored him.

I was completely reconciled to having crushes that never turned into reality, and of course it was much less troublesome to integrate a secret passion into the family routine. But for once my yearning and gazing actually had a tangible result. The love of punk rock that I shared with Mark Sykes brought us sweetly together.

I was as passionate about punk as it was possible to be whilst still having neat bobbed hair and wearing outfits from Dorothy Perkins. In fact virtually the only thing that betrayed my love of the Clash, the Gang of Four, the Buzzcocks and all the other jerky boys was my wearing of two small Tom Robinson Band badges. No black eyeliner ever streaked up towards my hairline, no safety pins were ever jabbed into my skin (except possibly when I was trying to keep up the cheap zip on my too-tight jeans). My entire love affair with New Wave was a secret.

The cause of my secretiveness was my dad's loathing of pop music. It enraged him, and he wanted me to feel the same way he did. He even made me promise that if I ever felt the urge to buy a pop record I would tell him and he would *pay* me the price of the record *not* to buy it. But it was no good. His strategy didn't work – I had to have vinyl. Now, more than anything, I needed vinyl that would impress Mark Sykes.

Part of my secret punk life involved waiting in the front room every Thursday morning to catch the moment of delivery of my copy of the *NME* (so that I could keep it out of Dad's sight). Then I would read it closely, absorbing its information and opinions wholesale, and, in particular, scanning the smudgy listings of records for sale by mail order from Rough Trade Records, the coolest record shop in the country. And once I had ordered something from them I again had to spend every morning before school hovering in the cold front room, watching through the net curtains for the postman so that I could take delivery of my new LP without anyone else being any the wiser.

The day that *Inflammable Material*, the first LP by Stiff Little Fingers, was delivered, I took it to school in its fibrous Rough Trade packaging – even that was cool. I sat with it in the sixth-form common room during a free period and Mark Sykes came in and asked me what it was. I drew out the glossy black sleeve and handed it to him like an offering. He took the disc out and put it on the feeble record player that we were allowed to have in the common room. Then, with only me watching, he played air guitar to the crashing chords, using the record sleeve as his imaginary Fender. Oh it was cool, alright, of course it was. It might not have been cool if anyone else had been doing it, but Mark Sykes playing air guitar was cooler than Mick Jagger in a stretchy one-piece. The delicate way his index finger and thumb held the imaginary plectrum; the way his wrist bent to let the plectrum twang the guitar strings; the way his head was turned away just so, eyes fixed on the middle distance, because *he* didn't need to look at the strings to play the chords just *perfectly*; the way the turn-ups on his black school trousers encircled the toes of his ever-so-slightly platform-soled school shoes. When I got the sleeve back, it was covered with sweaty finger- and thumb-prints, the laminated surface permanently dulled. But they were *his* fingerprints and they recorded those few minutes of perfect happiness.

My involvement with Mark after that was fluid and unspecific. He was, maybe, too grown-up for conventional going out. I thought he was wonderful, but I was also afraid of having a boyfriend, terribly afraid of what it would make me turn into in my parents' eyes. We didn't do any routine girlfriend-boyfriend things, going for walks, sitting in cafes, going to the pictures. I didn't have the well-developed sense of what 'going out' entailed that other teenagers had. I didn't read *Jackie* or go to the youth club at school. I hadn't got that feeling of entitlement which is perhaps the marker of the true teenager, but had rather continued to feel exactly as I always had, a child, getting physically bigger but not really any more adult. This is surely at the heart of everything: Mark had to be an underground boyfriend because there was only any place for him in my secret life. He could only be accommodated in the split-off part of my life that loved frowned-on pop music, that read porn, that fantasised, that was not under the psychological dominion of my parents. It isn't a question of what they would or would not have allowed me to do. The taboos under which I operated were so strong that I never tested what I could 'get away with', apart from once.

One day, after school, a singular day never to be repeated, I took Mark up to my bedroom. I don't know where our lust had welled up from because we had barely touched each other up till then. On my bed with the collapsing springs that rolled you into its middle like a boat, I lay down and undid my nylon school blouse. Mark lay down too, the combination of gravity and the steep gradient ensuring that we were tightly packed together. Although I have the clearest memory of being there with Mark, part of what I remember is a mental blankness, an emotional absence which must have been how I dealt with my transgression. It was a way of doing something whilst seeming not to do it and it allowed me to push on into new lands where sex was made of hot, hard flesh rather than paper.

We groped each other muskily and, bolder than I had ever

been before, I undid his school-uniform trousers and, after fumbling rather desperately with the waistband of his underpants, grasped his erection. I think I even looked at it, momentarily. (This glimpse was to take on more and more significance as the years went by and I realised that it was perfectly possible to have a sexual relationship with a man and never actually look their penis in the eye.) That first contact with human flesh swollen to the rigidity of a young branch, but warm, interactive, could only have astonished me. What did I do with it? I had no idea *what* to do with it beyond a primitive instinct to *grip* it. Then, as though caused by the act of gripping, I heard the back door opening, just below my bedroom window, and my mother *cooee*-ing her usual hello. She was a teacher at my school so it was normal for her to get home not long after me, but I hadn't taken that into account. My hand sprang away from Mark's cock as if it had been scorched. I was instantaneously upright, buttoning up my blouse at the same time as wiping my hand on the synthetic fabric, which crackled with static like a radio about to broadcast my secrets. *Shit!* I ran-walked downstairs and greeted mum.

'Hi! Nice day at school?' This was me to her.

'Yes. You?'

I heard the lavatory flush upstairs and started trying to think of what I could say to make this screaming abnormality of a boy upstairs in our house seem of little or no note.

'Oh, yeah, erm, Mark's, er, come home with me.' *My face blazing, blood singing at my temples.* 'He's just going.'

'Right. Hello, Mark.'

Mark came down the stairs, perhaps feeling slightly dizzy at the brutal rapidity of his ejaculation and his immediate subsequent ejection from our house. 'Hello, Mrs Jones.'

I opened the front door and he went down the stone steps

and out of the gate. Nothing more was ever spoken about what had just happened, by him, by me, by my mother. She seemed not to be concerned, barely even to have noticed him. In my desperation to avoid having to discuss it, I was glad to go along with this nonchalance, which I don't even think was feigned: it was only me who had the hang-up about boyfriends, born out of the distorted taboos that underlay my parents' relationship to each other and to me. That was all hidden deep below, where it would have taken psychotherapy to dig it all out. On the surface there was a normality which would have permitted me to have a boyfriend if I had just had the courage to try one on for size.

That was the first moment in my life when my desire crept out and engaged with another human being. My feelings for Mark had overcome all my reticence and sense of taboo and I was actually doing something straightforwardly sexual. Whether I was *enjoying* it is another question entirely.

When my mother arrived home and interrupted my intimacy with Mark, it felt as though a brave experiment had to be abandoned, the shock of failure so terrible that no further attempts could be sanctioned. Reality played no part: the fact that my mum might have been expected to come home just then, as she almost always did, the fact that we could have arranged another tryst the very next day if we had wanted to. None of this figured. No, it would be unseemly to repeat the scenario. Rolling around on my bed with Mark Sykes was so dreadful that retribution in the form of my mother had inevitably come down upon me. The acute embarrassment I felt as Mark jogged down the stairs ensured that my sexual desire went underground and stayed there. To anyone else, what happened that afternoon might have been taken in their stride, laughed off, a teenage escapade. For me, I wonder whether it was more catastrophic, whether the processes of maturing, of self-discovery and the discovery of boys' bodies were interrupted and never really resumed.

If I think more broadly about shame, for that is really what is at issue here, my memory jumps to one or other of several shameful incidents: the only time I ever had to stand behind my chair at school – purportedly for deliberately dropping a pencil on the floor so that I could look up the teacher's skirt as I bent to retrieve it; the time, a few years later, when I was the caller in a game of decimal bingo and pee-ed on the floor in front of the whole class because there didn't seem any way to interrupt the game to go to the loo (my mother was called to take me home, which seems an excessive reaction); the time I was ticked off by a prefect because I'd told on him for smoking. None of these events seems particularly shameful now, but in each case the memory consists more of revisiting the feelings of guilt and ignominy rather than just remembering what happened. Those feelings, when fresh, scored deep trenches which I would do anything to avoid falling into again. So it was with the Mark incident.

It was so much safer to remain childish, to endlessly repeat the small acts of goodness which brought me approbation, the pleasure of a good mark and praise for it. There was no uncertainty about coming first in an exam, about getting twenty out of twenty in a test, or getting an A on my homework (except that it *could* have been an A+). All my life – and it's no different now – I have not only loved to win praise but I need it. A job where I am my own boss and get to make decisions myself only makes me feel adrift and futile: how much more fulfilling it would be to have a wonderful boss to impress with my creativity and flair. That's the child in me who still wants to make Daddy happy and get extra pocket money for being a good girl.

A good girl does not overthrow her parents by becoming adult herself. If sex is a problem in a family rather than a straightforward source of joy, then one way to deal with it is to deny its existence, for everyone to be infantilised. But whilst I ostensibly played along with this (my psychological survival seeming to depend on it), my sexual side was busily seeding itself beneath the soil, and the more it developed, the greater the pressure between my two personae grew.

The afternoon with Mark happened during the term when we took our A-levels. School ended early for us and after the exams there was a long summer of nothing much except waiting for real life to start. I had already arranged to spend the coming year as an au pair in Paris, before going to university. In the mean time I spent my days lying on a brown corduroy mattress in the back garden reading Evelyn Waugh and Robert Graves and Aldous Huxley.

It must have been universally acknowledged that Mark Sykes was a 'grown man' and not some mere schoolboy for as soon as school finished he was selected to be a member of the jury for a big murder trial miles away. For the two weeks of the trial he travelled back from the court every evening and, no doubt drained by the grim evidence he had been asked to consider, called at our house to see me.

I should have been thrilled; any normal girl would have been. To have lovely, handsome Mark Sykes coming to see you devotedly, day after day, like a *proper boyfriend*, should have been all I could have wanted. But picture the three of us, my mum, dad and me, in the gloom of the telly room (my mother never liked to put a lamp on until it was actually dark), Mum and Dad in their separate armchairs, dozing, me crouched on the stool. We were like mantelpiece ornaments, comfortable in our familiar and unchanging relation to each other, lifeless.

Whenever our doorbell rang, the first response was always fear. Someone was trying to get in, someone would see us, see us vegetating in front of the television, understand from a mere sight of the triptych all that was wrong in our family. The ring of the bell was like a camera flash going off, the moment of capture.

The first time Mark came, I wasn't expecting him. When I opened the front door and saw him there I was shocked. What was I going to do with him? He seemed to fill the doorway, and he looked so *adult* in his smart juryman clothes. I just couldn't imagine taking him inside where the clammy mist of our life swirled in every room. Making a decision on the spot, I pulled the door closed behind me and we walked along the road to a bench overlooking the town. I can't remember what we did there, whether we held hands, kissed, how long we stayed out. All I remember is awkwardness and self-consciousness. I imagined my mum and dad wondering what I was doing when I failed to return from answering the door (though I don't suppose they spoke to each other about it). Their abandoned forms, unmoving in their comfy chairs, held greater sway over me than Mark himself.

It must be a mark of my self-absorption that, until I came to write this account, three decades after the event, I never wondered about the nature of the crime on which Mark, eighteen, was called to pass judgement. He certainly never broke the confidentiality under which he was bound when he came straight from the court sessions to see me. I noticed, for the first time, that in my diary for 1979 I actually wrote down the name of the case: 'the Miriam Culine murder'. There is nothing beyond the victim's name but it means I knew he was having to consider a murder. And the form of words suggests that at the time it had a significant degree of notoriety. In the years that followed I developed a strong interest in true crime, reading hundreds of books, publishing accounts of crimes as part of various jobs in the book industry and even ending up one year as a judge for the leading true-crime book prize. Yet I seem to have had a complete failure of imagination with regard to what Mark must have been going through at that trial. The 'crime' of his penetrating our family tomb, Howard Carter-like, was so shocking and had to be dealt with so immediately, that every other reality was pushed away. Curses had been released.

Miriam Culine (as she became) was the daughter of a Pentecostal pastor who went to a private school and seemed to have a conventional life mapped out for her by her parents. But at the age of seventeen she ran away with Fred Culine, forty years older than herself and a member of a well-known family of travelling showmen. Fred ran a fairground rodeo while Miriam worked on the family's candy floss stall, earning the nickname 'Candy Floss Queen'. They didn't actually marry until eighteen months before Miriam was murdered at the age of thirty-three. Perhaps the act of marriage was an attempt to shore up a relationship that was already crumbling. When Miriam's body was found, dreadfully burned, in the burnt-out remains of her car, police arrested Lawrence Wood, another Traveller, with whom she had been having an affair. But Wood was acquitted of the murder (thanks in part, then, to Mark) because the jury must have believed his claim that the affair had finished months previously when Miriam's husband found out about it. Lawrence Wood had been helping her plan an escape from the fairground and had been selling her belongings for her to raise money for her new life; she thought he would come with her but in fact he already had a new girlfriend. Miriam must have been heartbroken and very afraid. Her husband took out a life-insurance policy on her, for a term of only six months, and it was due to expire a few weeks after her death, but no one else was ever arrested for Miriam's murder.

The story of the Candy Floss Queen speaks to me: the pathos of a young woman who, having acted out a fantasy of running away to join the circus, found herself trapped in a hard life with a husband grown old, holding out hope of another fantasy escape with her lover. It's a story I can readily bring to life in my imagination, putting faces to the players, costuming them, filming them in my head. And I can also imagine, now, the strangeness, the horror even, of an eighteen-year-old schoolboy confronted with forensic evidence – including, no doubt, photographs of the burnt-out car, of the body – and forced to sit on the hard jury bench and listen to hard men explaining their part in a murdered woman's life. Back then, Mark's days at the trial were absent from my thoughts. If anyone was on trial, it was me.

It was the end of June and my seventeenth birthday was coming up. Sweetheart that he was, Mark kept calling every evening, and I knew that he would want to mark it in some way – he was my boyfriend, and that's what boyfriends do. I was determined to prevent this. Any special occasion where interest was focused on me alone – gifts, cards, visible expressions of affection – caused me intense anxiety. Perhaps what I was afraid of was seeming to set myself up as a rival to my mother for men's attention.

On the afternoon of my birthday, before Mum and Dad came home from work, I filled a carrier bag with a drink, a packet of crisps, a novel, paper and a pen and stuffed it into the tartan vinyl zip-up basket on the back of my bike.

This bike was the first one I had ever owned and had been given to me by my dad the previous Christmas as a special reward for getting into Cambridge. Every Cambridge student has a bicycle, as we knew, so the gift of the bike was supposed to encapsulate the glory of the old University and my success at getting a place there – it stood for *Brideshead Revisited*, punts on the Cam, dappled sunlight on old stone, gowns billowing behind carefree students as they cycled to lectures – but it was the *wrong* bicycle. It had half-sized wheels with white rubber treads. Something about the handlebars meant that the rider had to sit perkily upright. And that tartan *thing* on the back. Even I knew that the right sort of bicycle was a big black one, preferably old and dented, with a wicker basket on the front. When I had been presented with the bike at Christmas (and it had been a big deal; although secondhand, the bike had been buffed up, the white wheels scrubbed, the zip-up basket Jiffed), I had hated it on sight, but I had had to pretend to be overwhelmed by it and its Romantic significance. I hadn't ridden it since, but now it would come into its own as a getaway vehicle.

I wheeled the bike out of the garage and got self-consciously onto the saddle. I barely knew how to ride a bike because I'd never been allowed to have one as a child. I folded my feet up onto the pedals and flapped away, out of the back alley, up the hill and out of town.

That afternoon is achingly clear in my memory. The bright sky, the smell of mown hay, the long pull up the hill (the bike had no gears) and my Jesus sandals lightly scraping the tarmac with each turn of the pedals. My face was rigid with determination. I had no plan; I was just following an impulse – a very childish impulse for someone who had just turned seventeen – to run away.

The houses went on for about a mile, first the Thirties semis, then the clusters of Sixties development. The hill levelled out and the fields began. I saw a gate and stopped. I hauled the bike through the gate and out of sight. Then I sat down just inside the field and leaned against the dry-stone wall. I had never done anything like this before and it was out of character because, having played alone in fields as a small child, by now I had come to be afraid of being out in fields on my own. In spite of the loveliness of the day and the green quiet of the field I felt nervous. I got out my book and read for a while. I wrote a letter to my French penfriend, the usual stiff sentences about my likes and dislikes, polite wishes for her happiness. *"J'espère que tu vas passer une belle vacance."* I didn't mention that I had gone into hiding to avoid the attentions of my suitor. I ate the crisps and drank the pop. I tried to maintain a mental blankness, fending off thoughts of Mark arriving to find me not there. In the end I was just waiting for time to pass, not existing. Not existing is useful. When I thought I must have hidden out for long enough, I cycled home again.

It was around eight o'clock. I hadn't told anyone where I was going, but nobody was usually bothered about that. Surely by now Mark would have been to the house, been told that I was out, and would have gone away? When I went in through the back door, the house was springy with a strange energy. My mother was in the kitchen making a pot of tea.

'Where've you *been*? Mark's in the drawing room waiting for you.'

So I had failed. I went down through the house and opened the door into the front room. Incredibly, it was warm; even in summer this room was never naturally warm. *The gas fire was on* – unheard of except for the visits of very elderly aunts. Steadfast Mark Sykes was sitting on the pink plush sofa, a wilted rose nodding in his hand. On the floor by his feet three small plates were lined up, each with an empty Kitkat wrapper, and three empty cups – the good ones. Mum came in with his fourth cup of tea.

'Poor Mark's been here absolutely ages.' Her eyes mugged desperation at me. 'Where on earth have you been?'

I shrugged. 'Sorry.'

When she'd gone, he gave me the sad rose and a present. It was a really cool record (the *Cold City* EP by Spizz Oil), way too cool for me. There was nothing to say. It was so obvious I had been trying to avoid him and that meant I Wanted To Finish. I didn't want to; part of me just wanted to kiss him and sleep with him and be in love with him, but another part of me wanted a quick end to the tension and the worry, the weirdness of not being my mother's little companion any more. I let the awkwardness go on for a few minutes and the scene swiftly came to its inevitable conclusion. He was sad – or was he angry? He was *emotional*, that's for sure; some big slab of dignified male feeling was standing like a gravestone in his chest. But he didn't make a big thing of it. Mark Sykes left my house, and I never saw him again.

Chapter 3

STORIES OF OW

Athens is an equisite city. It is the capital of Greece. Below is a map of Athens.

The Acropolis which is a huge outcrop of rock above Athens is on the left-hand bottom corner of the map ... Above the stadium to the left are the beautiful National Gardens where I once got lost with my mother...

In Athens there is a large hill at the top of which there is a tiny church and a lovely café. To get to the top you can walk but you are more sensible if you ride in the funicular railway which is an electic train which travels up very steep gradients. At the top you get the most wonderful view of Athens laid out before you. There is a telescope for seeing father away.

School project on Greece, 1973 (age 10)

ALTHOUGH I was born in 1962, well into the age of modern technology, I had the childhood of an earlier time. Through me, my mother staged a re-run of her own childhood in the Thirties, which in turn had replicated that of *her* mother. As a girl Mum had been constantly sent out on errands around the marketplace, where they lived above their shop, the Bazaar – to the wet fish shop for cod tails, to the butcher's for chops, and of course for bread and milk daily. So when she found herself in charge of our household she had no thought of doing the shopping weekly, as others did, but would send me along to the dirty little shop at the end of the road on last-minute missions to get items – *crucial* items – for whatever meal she was about to tackle.

Such was my father's distress if a meal was not on the table at the prescribed time – his cry of "Me belly thinks me throat's cut!" would be only the overture to a whinge of operatic proportions – that we always seemed to be on the point of disaster, but we were simply living according to the rhythms of an earlier time. If the corner shop was shut I would have to go further afield in search of eggs or a tin of Tyne Brand steak – to the shop up on the council estate (discouragingly known as Cutpurse) or, on half-day closing, to the inferior supermarket at the far side of the market square, shunned at all other times but the only shop open in the whole town on Wednesday afternoons.

There was another way in which my mother transferred the habits of an earlier time into my upbringing: she did not consider it any sort of risk to let me out by myself from around the age of five. Apart from my vital shopping errands, if I was out finding my own entertainment then she could immerse herself in her own affairs: her reading, her writing, her painting. This would have been less significant if I had had brothers and sisters, or a gang of friends to go around with, but I was a very solitary single child. (As a child my mother had played out with all the other children, having the run of the whole town and the surrounding fields, woods and riverside. I'm sure she imagined I would find a similar society out in the streets. She seems to have idealised her role as 'gang leader', to have found, as a child, her perfect self-image: a tough and adventurous pirate queen with a following of younger kids who would hang on her every word when she ordered a raid or, when they were tired, listen enthralled to the fantastic stories she made up. When she had me, she had a gang again.)

The first outings I can remember were to the sweet shop at the bottom of Jail Bank (another grimly criminal street name).

Carrie Jones

There was no pavement on the bank and cars would go by fast, flying down the steep hill as I pressed myself in against the high limestone walls which enclosed a market garden on the slope. I would have a few pennies in my pocket to spend on jelly worms, candy prawns and flying saucers – my father called all these generic penny sweets '*ket*', a north-east dialect word which comes from the Old Norse for carrion but now just means 'rubbish'. I was a terrible snob myself from the earliest age and had strong views on books and films and TV programmes as well as my own taxonomy of sweeties. This boiled down to a simple premise: the ones *I* bought were acceptable, whilst there were other ones that were 'common' and bad for you – these included Blackjacks and Fruit Salads, Drumsticks, gobstoppers and sweet tobacco.

Sometimes my parents spent Sunday afternoon at the tennis club (which was not at all grand, just two courts squeezed into a tiny plot) and while they played, I would go across the road and over the fence to play alone in the immense field which had been used for strip farming in medieval times. Straggly hawthorn hedges still marked the boundaries of some of the ancient plots, and I loved to make a home for myself in the dusty, scooped out hollows beneath their exposed roots. I was never afraid; the possibility that I might be afraid never cropped up. I was very very happy making cupboards and larders and bathrooms and bedrooms for hours. I don't think I ever saw anybody else there, and if I had I wouldn't have been afraid.

The town did have its own bogeyman, Dirty Ernie, who really was frighteningly mad with a blackened, snarling face and an unnaturally fast, loping stride. He was dangerous, especially when drunk, and was regularly locked up for periods of time. My mother once saw him running along the top of a row of parked cars. Yet the idea that Dirty Ernie was at large and might harm me never seemed to occur to anyone. At one time he had a job with the Council as a road-mender – that was when he tried to run me over with the roller he was using to tamp down fresh tarmac in the churchyard. My route to school went through the churchyard – sometimes I would go off the path to see the grave where a man's leg was buried in 1606, alongside the rest of his body, which died nine years later. The leg was lost when its owner fell over a local escarpment while on horseback. He famously hacked open the body of his dead mount and pushed his broken legs inside to save himself from hypothermia, but one leg didn't make it. There was also a mass grave of plague victims in the churchyard. It was a merry place.

So, when did fear come? Perhaps it was hormonally imprinted in my body while I was in the womb, but simply took a while to show itself. My mother likes to recount how she was in an extremely nervous state all through her pregnancy: her mother used to vet the newspaper every day and cut out stories which she thought would be too disturbing. If anything escaped censorship and my mother got upset she would be unable to eat for days. Mum also took Thalidomide for morning sickness while she was carrying me and, although I was luckily spared any physical disfigurement, I've always wondered if it played any part in my subsequent development – a lot of Thalidomide children were of above-average intelligence, although I don't believe the part the drug may have played in this has yet been fully understood. I'm not claiming genius, but I'm quite different in character from the rest of my wider family and was the first one to continue on to university after school.

But if fear was washed into me as my cells divided in the terror-soup of my mother's uterus, for years and years I had no fear of my environment. I felt completely safe in the town and in the surrounding countryside. My father, however, seemed to think that it was necessary for a child to feel some fear and so he set up various scary situations in order to toughen me up. He liked to make me hold things while he drilled or sanded them with power tools – the idea was that I should not flinch from the big, wet-looking sparks fountaining out from the drill-head or sanding disc. Of course I used to scream and scream. He also used to run his lighter up and down my shins – he maintained that there was no need to be afraid because the flame is always drawn to the vertical and so doesn't burn. The smell of singed hair suggested otherwise, but it was true that it didn't hurt, though it still made me scream. I was never quite sure whether the screaming was fun or not.

Another way my dad scared me was Death Alley. Every Saturday, having spent all day at his mother's, we would drive home – a journey of about ten miles. Death Alley was my name for the long, curving road down from the dual carriageway to the last village before home. Perhaps my father's longing for death was intensified by the long, boring hours spent with his difficult mother. He would always accelerate wildly down the hill, faster and faster; the headlights of oncoming cars would veer past, occasionally we would hear the dying blare of a horn. He never wore his safety belt and, as I cowered in the back and willed him to slow down, he would go even faster and shout out that the NHS could bloody well fork out for an accident as he'd been paying into it for umpteen years. I have an idea that he used to turn the car headlights off as well, but that may be imagination.

Mum says that if I fell over and hurt myself and she comforted me, he would become enraged, especially if she murmured, 'There, there.' He couldn't bear to hear 'There, there.' Mum, for her part, used to borrow again and again a particularly sentimental book from the library, about a boy called Soldier and a bear, because she liked to watch my eyes brimming over with tears each time I read it.

Without making it seem too *Grand Guignol*, I believe I fulfilled needs for my parents that they failed to provide for each other. Where there was an absence of intimacy and shared pleasure, of legitimate transgression as part of the excitement of sex, those impulses were blocked and diverted. Instead they turned to the services of affection and mirroring that could be rendered by a compliant and loving child.

Perhaps it seems contradictory that a child could spend a great deal of time alone and yet also claim to have been exploited by her parents (albeit at a subconscious level). But although I was often out of sight and out of mind, when I did enter the orbit of one or other of my parents, I became an *aspect* of them. This was particularly the case with my mother. I was never a presence in my own right — never just a big, ungainly nuisance making my own noises and messes and demanding to be fed or entertained. I have my own children now and their capacity to be themselves — loudly, cheerfully, endlessly — astonishes me. When I say to them, 'I never ever dropped my clothes on the floor' or 'I wasn't allowed to say I was bored,' they just look at me and then carry on.

When I was in my teens my mum and I often chose the exact same clothes or the same shoes. This wasn't Boden-style cuteness on my mother's part, it was more that what she liked was what I liked and vice versa — we both had identical navy-blue suits, the same wedge shoes, the same mac. It was as if the boundaries between us didn't exist, everything could pass between us — or at least from her to me. Nothing was taboo:

bodily functions, the symptoms of illnesses, her fears and embarrassments. It didn't seem weird or unhealthy. We had a laugh, lots of laughs, even when my dad was in a bad mood, which he often was. Together the two of us could ward off unhappiness by laughing at his tempers or making secret faces at him. And I made quite a good husband substitute from an early age – looking after the tickets and passports when we went on holiday (he never came), making sure we changed trains at the right station, being good company and sitting on my mum's knee until I was a huge near-adult about to leave home.

I had once spent a great deal of time on my dad's knee too, when I was much younger and before the awkwardness set in. In fact I would often spend the evening being enticed from one lap to the other and back again, and I wonder if there was some sort of competition going on for who could keep me the longest.

This begins to explain how, at seventeen, I was so hung up about admitting my interest in boys that I froze out the perfect boyfriend. It would have been a form of adultery.

When I was only seven or eight, at the C of E Junior School, a boy in my class called Gordon (but nicknamed 'Cess' after his father, who was Cecil) took a shine to me. He brought me little presents such as a tiny torch and a grubby packet of Beechnut chewing gum (I was horrified to be given gum, which I knew was 'common' – you'd have thought he'd given me a wrap of cocaine). He even knocked on our door wanting to play with me, and I felt, for the first time, the hot burn of shame which was to ruin so many of my future contacts with the opposite sex. When a boy liked me, I felt as though *I* had done something forbidden and I felt guilty and ashamed. It was exactly the way I felt when I got a verruca once, even though that wasn't my fault either. The day after Cess came to the house, I took my revenge. When he came up to me in the playground I lunged forward and bit him hard on the knee.

All through my childhood I instinctively hid any interest in sex and boys. And I hid it successfully, I think, in spite of living my life under what seemed unusually close surveillance – though maybe that was just paranoia on my part. In one of my favourite children's books, *Lucky Les*, the hero cat Les saves an orchard from being stripped of its plump fruit by rigging up a television screen in every tree and then scaring away marauding birds by leaping and hissing in front of a camera wired to all the screens. That's how *my* life seemed: a vigilant aunt or great aunt in every tree, round every corner, and, later, in every pub and café, all eagerly reporting back to my mum and dad that I was growing up. And because Mum was a teacher at my comprehensive school, her influence was felt there too: the other teachers were her mates and would tell her they'd seen me holding hands with a boy as a cute morsel of gossip. But when *she* told it back to *me*, I would want to shrivel up. The only places I felt fully at ease were in my own house (*on my own*, which I seemed to be a lot of the time) and in my own head.

One of my very earliest memories is of a fantasy that I enjoyed when I was very very small, maybe three or four. I have never heard of anyone else with such fantasies, but perhaps they are simply unwilling to divulge them. Each night as I lay in bed I would settle down into the fantasy: that I was encased in a suit made of rubbery, stretchy material which would gradually fill with shit (well, in my head it was 'poo'). The poo would feel warm and good – not *at all* smelly. I think this must have been a memory of the liquid-filled container of my mother's womb and a longing for its safety.

As time went on, my fantasies continued to develop and

sub-divide. Nearly always involving restriction and swaddling, they retained their magic power to excite and reassure me for a long, long time. Over and over again, I would imagine my whole body being set in plaster of Paris or cemented up in a wall. Later, the fantasy was of being in a plane crash, trapped in the wreckage along with a boy – the only other survivor. This was perhaps at the age of seven or eight. I suppose the thing was that if the nice feelings were the by-product of calamity I would be absolved from guilt for feeling them. (I have always been fascinated by stories of survival after terrible disaster and can remember avidly reading about plane-crash victims having to eat their dead fellow passengers to survive, in the serialisation of *Alive!* in the *Sunday Times* colour supplement a few years later.) It seems a long time since those fantasies were potent, and these days I'm usually too exhausted to slip into fantasy. The fleeting scenes of abuse that occasionally flicker through my brain, the elaborate ceremonies, the hierarchies of men, the crude restraints, are surely quite closely related to those first childish scenarios and only altered by knowledge of the world.

There was another long-lived fantasy, which evolved into a game. After I had gone to bed, I would throw all the bedcovers off (needless to say my bedroom was incredibly cold as we only had gas fires in the downstairs rooms – no central heating for us in those days), pull my nightie up under my armpits and curl up in a ball, sometimes on the bed, sometimes on the floor. I was a poor orphan living on the streets, freezing near to death like the Little Match Girl. It was pure Victorian melodrama. Then a kindly gentleman (no doubt in a stove-pipe hat) would find me and give me a ragged dress with which to cover myself – at this point the nightie was pulled back down over my goose-pimpled legs. Later the philanthropist returned, this time with a thin blanket, and I would wrap myself in my brushed-cotton sheet. His drip-drip bounty would continue until I was living in gilt-and-plush splendour in the gentleman's own home – and fully wrapped in all my blankets again. In reality, it was almost impossible to get warm again unless someone had remembered to do me a hot-water bottle.

A little later, when I was nine or ten, I stopped relying only on my own imagination and started to mine other sources of stimulation.

For years and years my mum used to give me a rolled-up copy of *Private Eye* in my Christmas stocking and my dad a copy of *Mayfair*. I was far too young for *Private Eye*; I barely understood the cartoons, let alone the political satire and gossip. I don't know why she thought I would enjoy it. However, I was fascinated by *Mayfair*. My dad would unfurl the magazine, give a special little theatrical cough and say something loaded with false jollity and lubricity: '*Ahem*, I'll enjoy that later, very nice too…' It was the only explicit reference to sexual pleasure that ever passed between my parents from one year to the next (unless you count the time when we were out in the car for the day and Dad made a joke about the road-sign for uneven road surface meaning 'brassieres in the road'). Why it survived when everything else died and fell away, I don't know.

When a family is slowly falling apart, celebrations are one of the first things to erode as it becomes impossible to maintain the ritual pretence of gaiety. We were never much good at doing Christmas in our house – when our threadbare tinsel tree came down from the attic once again, its wire branches succumbing to metal fatigue after so many years of folding down and folding up, it was hardly 'Deck The Halls'. The signifiers of Christmas persisted, but they were strangely altered. It was fun to hunt for my presents before they appeared under the tree; not so fun to find *two* of everything. My dad had bought the same things – sweets, puzzles, annuals – for my mum's friend's daughter as he had for me, signalling his own growing closeness to Mum's friend. I felt that the specialness of the presents was largely cancelled out by their being duplicated for another girl, but in other ways I profited from Dad's friendship with her mother: when I began to go round to play at her house (at a certain point our getting together was perhaps subtly fomented), he would come to collect me, but the play dates extended long into the evening until I was finally tired and keen to go home. The food at her house was delicious and plentiful – soon I was eating several meals a week there, served on a little occasional table as I sat on the sofa watching *Follyfoot* or *The Double Deckers*.

Dad always hid his Christmas porn mag under the sofa cushions, gritted with shreds of his pipe tobacco. When I found myself on my own I would get it out and lie on my stomach on the sitting-room carpet to leaf through it. The pin-ups were good because taboo. I knew it was wrong wrong wrong to peer with such interest at the stubble poking up around the edges of their straining scanties, or to see the sun shining through their fluffy pubic hair, usually bleached to a light ginger (hairlessness in pornography was not the rule back then but only an extra-kinky option). I wasn't very interested in their heavy, swollen breasts, but I liked the self-conscious positions they were made to lie in, showing the forbidden parts of their bodies whilst they concentrated on gazing dreamily into the middle distance. Better than the pictures were the words, in particular the readers' letters with their cartoonish accounts of sex in Ford Cortinas, sex with the window-cleaner (those *Confessions* movies were hot at the time), sex with teacher, sex on the golf course… Did I get turned on? Sort of, there was definitely a throbbing in the pit of my stomach, but I was perhaps more aroused by the forbidden act of reading this stuff than by the content itself. Yet, already, the distinction was blurred. It disturbs me to think how young I was when this tendency began to show itself, and I blame my early enjoyment of the feeling of 'badness' when reading porn for my later propensity to be unmoved, left cold, by tenderness. Long before I started having sex myself, I had this knowledge of a particular version of it – exaggerated, boastful, mine's-bigger-than-yours *bonking*. That's what I thought sex would be like, *wanted* it to be like. But, in my experience, nice, ordinary sex isn't like that, being more like a Coldplay album: sincere, a bit earnest, not too long.

I failed to connect the feelings aroused in me by looking at soft porn with the possibility of real sexual stimulation. In those days there were no images of women masturbating in *Mayfair*, and I had only the vaguest idea that such a thing was a possibility and that it might feel nice. Once or twice I remember lying on my stomach in bed with a finger very cautiously placed just inside my vagina, *only just*, and quite quite still, as I waited for something, who knew what, to happen. Naturally nothing did. It seems odd that I could know enough to do this and yet have no idea that you needed to go on, so much further, on and on and on, but that perseverance would be fabulously rewarded. I did not persevere but soon matter-of-factly withdrew the finger and got on with reading my Puffin.

There was only so long that I could sustain my interest in the same old copy of *Mayfair*, and anyway, after a few months, each one would quietly disappear, and my dad and I would have to await a new one, come Christmas. Lucky (or unlucky) for me, then, that I found more reading material to hand. In a drawer in one of the spare rooms were not one but *two* copies of *The Story of O*, among a mass of old paperbacks. Some of these old books had come to us from my maternal grandmother, and I guess that, amazingly, one of these copies of the most controversial pornographic novel of the day once belonged to Granny. Hers must have been the one carefully covered with brown paper to disguise its corrupting cover. I love the idea of her sitting with this hand-grenade of a book, neatly folding and taping the brown paper onto it, as if that made it all right to have it in the house. (Granny was an unorthodox woman in her Brutus denim jacket and leopard-print ski pants. She used to play the electric organ at family get-togethers, her massive gold charm bracelet rattling against the keyboard.)

The Story of O, purportedly written by a woman, Pauline Réage, was, it later turned out, more conventionally written by a man. O is a girl, whose hollow name brilliantly encodes not only her emotional emptiness but also the steel ring that enslaves her and the sexual 'holes' which ultimately define her. She becomes the willing and totally submissive slave of an aristocratic *milord* who provides her with a secret life-outside-life at his chateau, where she is repeatedly flogged and sodomised.

O quickly became something of an obsession. I became fixated on it because it was clearly a really *bad* book, about subjects that went way beyond the cheerful laddishness of *Mayfair*. And it was in *my* house! It made me feel that I had power over my parents, because I knew about their possession of this proscribed book, and also because I was able to read it without their knowledge. The story itself didn't do much for me. I hated the painful bits. What I liked was the way that O relinquished control over her life: it was being holed up in a wall all over again. I also loved all the sections where O was groomed for her new life of sexual servitude, with maids picking over her body and bathing and dressing her. This I lifted wholesale into my own fantasies, leaving the chains and whips behind. Very many of my sexual fantasies since this key seeding period have seen me either immobilised, or voluntarily passive, willingly bound, 'taking it', so that I don't have to play any part in giving anyone else pleasure, or else removed from the sexual frenzy altogether, a pale imitation of the great Marquis himself, directing and controlling others. I might add that none of this, none whatever, has *ever* surfaced in the timid reality of my sex life. Except maybe a general passivity, easily mistaken for dull, English, middle-class hung-up-ness.

When the car mysteriously arrives to take O to the chateau where she will be initiated into her new way of life, she allows herself to be borne away, without a struggle. She barely questions what is happening to her, and as time goes on no one seems concerned at her disappearance. How powerfully this appeals to me, and yet how terrifying the thought of it is! In one or two instances in my life I have, briefly, found myself in places where no one has known where I am (or only the person I am with), and I have had this sensation of being lost to the world – a mixture of exhilaration and the fear of annihilation.

Recently, never having owned my own copy of *The Story of O* and wanting to remind myself of what it was really like, I bought a copy on Amazon (wonderfully avoiding all embarrassment). The book when it came had a powerful hold over me. I couldn't bring myself to open it. Whereas once I had gone to it as soon as I was left alone, as other children might have sneaked to the sweetie jar, now I was fearful of what I would find in it. I wasn't so much afraid of the book itself as of discovering exactly what it was I had done to myself with it when I was so young. The English translation was first published in 1972, so I must have been nine or ten when I first read it. *O* must have been a *succès de scandale* when it first came out in this country, and I can picture my mother (and *her* mother) plucking up the courage to buy this tantalisingly wicked book after reading so much about it. I wonder if it was embarrassing for them to get their copies, or if the whole country went *O*-crazy and the taboo was overcome for a little while (as when Madonna published her *Sex* book)? Perhaps they asked a man to get it for them.

Re-reading *The Story of O*, after thirty years, I felt my child-self sidle up beside me and look over my shoulder. I was reading as an adult – just carefully working my way from beginning to end – but the sections which had obsessed me as a child sprang from the page still quivering with taboo eroticism, whilst the 'boring bits' that I'd once skipped over were still dormant, even though they were actually more important – the paragraphs which set out the book's philosophy of consensual abandonment of the self. It was a catalogue of all the erotic touchstones of my life. It seemed that every fantasy that had ever handed me into sleep had its source in these pages, every coincidental turn-on could trace its secret resonance back to *O*. I remember I once visited the Museum of Costume in Bath, as an adult, and saw a pair of eighteenth-century sheepskin leggings for a man, just two fleecy leg-shapes which would have left the genitals exposed. The excitement which they provoked in me was, I'm sure, a legacy of the aristos in *O*, with their violet robes and 'tights' which left their 'sex' free. It's laughable now, ridiculous, but it's imprinted on my imagination and can't be erased.

There are so many details which must have detached themselves from the narrative and lodged themselves like microbes in my mind: the rouged nipples and labia, the devices which were inserted into O to make her body more freely accessible. The arm of a chair over which O is bent, the hook on the wall by which she is held captive in her bed.

Now I don't know what to think. Is it shameful or cool to have *The Story of O* so deeply embedded in my head? Is it a strange thing to admit to, or nothing out of the ordinary? I just don't know. Was it damaging to read (and obsessively re-read) such a powerful book so young? For me it remains a treasure box which holds the 'magic stones' of my fantasy life.

When I was a child my most precious belonging was my treasure box. It was a square box made of stout cardboard with three little drawers. In the drawers I kept my treasures, which I would take out and examine nearly every day. I would sort them according to different categorisations – colour, size, or preference. I would look at them with the obsessive gaze of an autistic child. Quite a few were made of coloured glass, and I would hold these right up to my eye and stare at the light through them. When I started writing this book I went through the house looking for letters, diaries, notebooks, toys… everything I had kept from the past. I found my treasures, no longer in their original box, and I was shocked at how tawdry and broken they were. Two crumbling nuggets of purple quartz and a lozenge of purple cut glass ('amethysts' in my childhood gemmology), a couple of mother-of-pearl buttons, a scrap of glass from a chandelier, a plastic button with a Wedgwood-style cameo and 'Invitation to the Valse' in minute looping letters, a tiny blackened iron heart. These chipped and discoloured gewgaws had once been endlessly fascinating to me, but lost their magic once I looked at them with spoiled adult eyes.

The sexual treasures of *The Story of O* were more powerfully protected.

Chapter 4

AWFULLY HOT

After a fresh salad we all went down town. I saw all the boys in a bunch and for some reason rushed into a shop to avoid them. Suddenly I felt awfully hot and ill so I went home. Dad was a bit moody because I wouldn't go with him to the hardware shop.

Diary entry for April 20th 1976 (age 13)

NOBODY knew about my pornography habit, and nobody could ever have guessed, as in all other ways I was a *very* good little girl. I never brought what I'd learned from O and the various other bits of porn I'd found at home (none of which cast the same spell over me) into 'real life'. My erotic life was rigidly compartmentalised, separate and strictly imaginary. It didn't help that I was officially 'brainy', especially with the added affliction of being a teacher's daughter. Being brainy was a disaster as far as boys were concerned. Most teenage boys are not looking for an earnest bluestocking to be their girlfriend. But, even though I never skipped my homework and appeared to be a sexually inert lump in laddered tights, I was always smothered by crushes, pining for a look or a word from some schoolboy Adonis, and nearly always being passed over for someone else, usually my best friend, Caroline G. My crushes were breathy, innocent things, with handholding as the zenith of their hopes. Holding a boy's hand was the most exciting, sensual thing I could imagine actually doing myself, representing as it did the moment of declaration, of connection – the moment when the boy decided to make you his. But there was to be very very little handholding for me until the last years of secondary school. I had been badly put off in the first year, when Derek Allan held my hand on the way home from Joy-Seekers.

Joy-Seekers was a Christian 'club' which had been set up by some very enthusiastic sixth-form girls (in whom the spirit clearly moved, so shining were their eyes, so lustrous their long straight hair) and which tried to be jolly to disguise its evangelical agenda. My hometown was rife with Jehovah's Witnesses, Mormons, Pentecostalists and other sub-religions, and there was virtually no activity organised for young people which did not fall under the auspices of one of these groups. Instinctively atheistic, I was nonetheless lured into Joy-Seekers right at its inception. The bait was the competition the girls organised: come up with the best name for the new club and win the glory of having your name in lights – or rather in felt-tips, pinned on the Lower School noticeboard. Yes, 'Joy-Seekers' was *my* name. No doubt, at the time, the name seemed innocent and upbeat, a close relative of the New Seekers, our ambassadors at that year's Eurovision Song Contest and about as sunny a pop group as you could get. Now, it also has unwelcome sexual overtones, the inevitable result of reading too many French structuralists' essays about *jouissance*, the 'joy' of orgasm. (Even as I was joyfully throwing myself into 'big school', we first-year kids were galvanised by rumours that *dirty pictures* of the New Seekers were available for viewing in the coat room. I both wanted and didn't want to see these pictures, but curiosity won out, and I can remember a ripped-out magazine page with some hairy red-faced men standing in a line. The crime of pornography trespassing in school was so terrible that I hardly dared look at the crimson genitalia, but I'm sure it wasn't the New Seekers. Where was dreamy Lyn Paul, for a start?)

But walking up the hill from school with Derek Allan and him quite unexpectedly taking hold of my hand is a memory whose brightness puts Joy-Seekers into deep shade. I didn't have a crush on Derek. He was a heavy-set boy, with a big hooked nose and quite camp – nice, but not the stuff of my crushes. Yet when his fingers enlaced mine, that was serious! My hand suddenly felt like Popeye's, post-spinach: huge, hot, bursting with unnatural energy, shouting for attention. Look, LOOK, hand-*boy*-hand-*girl*, first time in history of universe, planet tilted from its axis, nothing the same again. But before I had time to begin to enjoy the weird sensation of being chosen, before I even arrived home, my Auntie Doris had *seen* us, and the event had been gleefully shared over the phone with my mother – not maliciously, I don't think it was ever malicious – so that when I *did* get home, my mum, smiling, was able to say, 'What's this I hear?', and I was frozen with shame and embarrassment.

For years after that I had very little physical contact with boys, even though there would always be someone whose name I repeated over and over in my mind like a mantra, willing him to appear as I walked down into town or along the short section of road which led to school. To see the Boy of the Moment coming down the road towards you was to experience a tumult of excitement that had to be very carefully contained. You would see the boy approaching; ideally he would be alone, but usually he would be with friends. If you were with *your* friend there would be the briefest whispered exchange, then highly disciplined silence. If you were alone, your eyes would rake the ground. You would *not* look up, *NOT* look up, as you felt the boy's presence move towards you, stirring the air, increasing the pressure of blood shunting in your ears. Then, if you got it just right, you would look up just as he was about to pass, and you would smile a very particular half-smile, almost apologetic, absolutely *no* teeth to be shown, then look down to the ground again. Once he had gone on behind you, you were permitted a gleeful grin, like that of a dog on a hot day. If you were with your friend you might laugh unnaturally loudly, in the hope that the boy would hear.

Nearly everything I did was a school activity. I went on school trips to see dozens of plays, which usually involved travelling quite long distances by coach. I adored these coach journeys, which often gave me more pleasure than the plays themselves. I liked to get a window seat, although this had to be negotiated with Caroline G – usually I got the window seat for one half of the trip only. It was best on the return journey, as then everyone would be tired and less inclined to talk. I liked to press my face to the glass and try to merge myself with the rushing lights outside. It was good if it was raining and the colours spangled and ran in the droplets. Sometimes the coach driver would play music on his 8-track (probably Elton John or Rod Stewart) and that made the experience even better, like being in a primitive pop video. Sometimes I would feel as though I had left my self behind entirely. I still love that feeling.

Once, on one of these return journeys, I heard a boy's voice barking my name from further up the bus. 'Oi! Caroline! Oi! Badger wants yer to sit next to him!' Did they mean me or Caroline G? They *always* meant Caroline G. She had proper breasts and permed hair. But, no, this time it was me. Badger was the nickname of a clever redheaded boy with whom I competed amiably but fiercely in Physics. I had a bit of a crush on Badger because of his brains, although his small, wiry frame wasn't my type. But still… Blushing, I lurched up the aisle and sat down heavily in the seat just vacated by Badger's friend and matchmaker, Dave 'Humpy' Hill. A cheerful shout of encouragement went up from the nearby seats and I was immediately engulfed in an inferno of self-consciousness. I sat absolutely still. So did he. The eight inches or so of his thigh touching mine seemed to be emitting an intense heat. The chatter of the other kids on the coach flared and faded in time with my thumping pulse, then the white noise in my head rose to drown out everything else until, at last, I flung myself back into my own seat and pretended to laugh about it with Caroline G.

It just seemed that I couldn't do straightforward boy/girl stuff. Even as I got older and became less prone to being overwhelmed by embarrassment (because by now I really wanted to do *stuff*), circumstances seemed to connive to trip me up.

A group of us went down to the new swimming pool during the holidays and had a highly charged time splashing and grabbing each other. Did I enjoy the sensation of being clutched from behind and held against a chubby boy's cold white stomach, feeling his trunks filling out against my bottom? His whole body felt like yeast-activated dough, rising and inflating. I liked the idea that I had *caused* the freaky swelling, but I didn't want to have to *engage* directly with it in any way. This moment was emblematic of my attitude towards the opposite sex. I thought it was both funny and rather awesome to see his nylon-clad stiffy, warped and magnified under the lapping water of the shallow end. And being the catalyst for the transformation of his flesh was a kind of magic. But I only wanted to see this evidence of my power, not touch. That hardened body part was surely unnatural, oedematous, and I instinctively shrank away from contact with it.

Cutting Up Playgirl

I had much warmer feelings for a different boy, feelings that were never complicated by visible erections. He was Jamie Callan, who played the clarinet next to me in the assembly orchestra. After a long, long crush, sustained by the pleasure of the intimate little hymn run-throughs we had every morning, I had really become quite devoted to him. Once I had even been invited to his house to play Monopoly and listen to his favourite record, 'Donna' by 10CC. He was part of the swimming-pool group that day, and afterwards, on the lazy walk home up the hill (*everywhere* in my hometown was at the top or bottom of a hill) he took my hand. *This* was the wondrous stuff of my fantasies, and I loved noticing the discreet reaction of the others as they took in our handholding and adjusted their mental card files to include this new 'official' pairing. But I had hardly begun to enjoy the feel of Jamie's fingers squeezing mine when the red suede Jesus sandals that I was wearing began to disintegrate as I walked along. With uncanny synchronicity, the stitching on the straps of both shoes just seemed to dissolve, and the soles began to slap noisily against my feet like clapperboards. I was like a circus clown. It was impossible to keep any dignity – it was virtually impossible to walk. The path was steep and rutted, un-made up, so I couldn't go barefoot. The romance of the handholding drained away and disappeared into the sharp stones. Once again I was smothered in hot embarrassment. Of course the thing with Jamie went nowhere after that.

Chapter 5

KISSING CAROLINE

'This song is one of our favourite songs and was written by S. Wonder and although he's blind he writes some of the most beautiful songs around. This one's called "You are the sunshine of my Lord".'

Script for a Belle Tones concert, 1975 (age 13)

SO what if I was a boyfriend-repelling disaster zone? I had an exclusively female club to share my secrets. And we were going to be famous! The Belle Tones was a singing girl-gang with a dress fund and rules – *lots* of rules. In charge of the Belle Tones was Nicola Kirby, in looks a slightly coarser version of Disney's Snow White. She had come to our town from the East End of London, but had fitted right in and was really popular. She was much more worldly than any of the natives – she knew all pop songs and could work out the chords to them on her acoustic guitar. She could draw strip cartoons just like the ones in *Jackie*, she could do that bulgy, overlapping lettering you got on the sleeves of *Top of the Pops* compilation LPs, and she wore foundation to cover her spots.

The line-up of the Belle Tones was, to put it mildly, fluid. At one point there were as many as seven members, but it wasn't a free-for-all – you did actually have to be able to sing (and not just tunes, either, but *parts*), and you had to be 'in' with the core members of the group: me, Nicola and Caroline G. It is probably true that we let some people join only in order to have the sour pleasure of kicking them out again when, inevitably, they displeased us. It was girl power before its time and ruthlessly wielded.

The Belle Tones sang Nicola's arrangements of David Cassidy and Carpenters hits, and more soulful songs such as 'Killing Me Softly' and 'After The Goldrush', 'I Believe' and Stevie Wonder's 'You Are the Sunshine of My Life'. It was all relatively sophisticated and we were particularly good at doing harmonies. It wasn't long before we were singing in assembly (and being quietly loathed by the whole school for our melodious talent). We wore matching full-length striped dresses which we had bought out of our earnings, singing in village halls for tiny branches of the Women's Institute (we asked for £9 for an evening's entertainment, and I often got the feeling that the ladies thought this was a bit steep, especially as we usually got a free pie-and-pea supper). These dresses were the cheapest we could find and made us look like a row of mock-Tudor villas when we lined up on stage. On other, less glamorous occasions, we wore grubby-looking white polo-necks and brown midi skirts, because that was the only outfit we could all cobble together without having to buy anything new. My jumper and skirt were borrowed from my Mum and made me feel middle-aged. We all wore ginger-tan wedgies made of leather so thin and inflexible that it was like wearing manila envelopes on our feet.

We used our Lorelei powers to seduce a boy on whom we all had a crush. Nicola worked out the first ever arrangement of a David Cassidy number for acoustic guitar and tuba. The boy in question was the tuba player in the school wind band and a large part of his attraction was the fact that his lips were permanently swollen into luscious crimson cushions from the huge effort of blowing into his massive instrument. There was also his abundant hair and affable good humour. Once we had worked out the song — and it had to be devilishly complicated for our special purposes — we told the tuba boy, Jem Stephenson, that we desperately needed his services for a new number we were about to start rehearsing, which, unusually, was arranged for tuba and guitar. Perhaps Jem suspected that he was being ensnared, but he turned up willingly enough at Caroline G's house one Sunday afternoon, looking only slightly bemused as he heaved his enormous tuba out of its black case. We were beside ourselves with excitement (there were four of us in the Belle Tones that week) and had to keep breaking off the rehearsal so that we could run into Caroline's kitchen and collapse in panting giggles. Nicola had composed the tuba part without any knowledge of the instrument's range or capabilities — she wanted Jem to play riffs with the same agility as she had strummed them on her guitar. He sounded like a whinnying llama as he gamely tried to reproduce the notes that Nicola played to him. Of course there was nothing written down. Between them, they worked out a slightly less frenetic version and then it was time to rehearse the voices. Jem absentmindedly massaged his still-vibrating lips as Caroline, Nicola, Karen Holmes and I started to build up the harmonies. When we got to the chorus, where we could let rip, it was as if we were singing to beautiful David himself. Jem's tumbling hair and smiley eyes morphed into the very essence of the angelic Cassidy. That afternoon was heaven. To have a nice boy entirely under our control was a delicious novelty. There wasn't even any sense of rivalry; we all shared our new possession.

Sadly, the magnificent arrangement of 'I Think I Love You' for tuba, guitar and female voices was never performed in public. In retrospect, it is clear that we were toying with Jem and we didn't have the nerve to lure him to one of our houses a second time, although he probably would have come. A little while later, at a very tame party thrown by Karen Holmes, Jem came and sat down next to me on the sofa, where I had been perched alone for a ridiculously long time. It seemed as though I was to be rewarded for my show of antisocial aloofness and I thrilled at how close he sat to me. He leaned in to my ear and spoke over the sound of The Osmonds' 'Love Me For A Reason': 'D'you think Caroline will go out with me?' Once again Caroline G's perky breasts, her constant applications of Charlie perfume and her orange-flavoured lip gloss had trounced my boyishly cropped hair and boyishly cropped chest. If *I* wore lip gloss it made my lips feel like slugs until I rubbed it off in irritation. There was no competition.

Me and Caroline G. The two Carolines. 'Like two peas in a pod,' people used to say. Bosom buddies. But really we were very unlikely best friends. For a start, only she had the bosoms; I was flat-chested, and for a long time it seemed that that was the chief difference between us. If a boy was going to fancy one of us, it would, *ipso facto*, be her. If two boys were hanging out with us, the one *I* liked was always the one that liked *her*, and that just had to be accepted. I remember once I ended up in the attic bedroom of one half of just such a pair of friends, in a rare and quite frenzied snogging session, while Caroline snogged *my boy* behind a beam. The whole episode would never have happened if I hadn't been with Caroline – she *enabled* it – but at the same time I was somehow the loser. I regretted kissing the consolation-prize boy.

The thing about Caroline G was that she only became my friend at secondary school. Caroline and I had never played dolls together or built a den or played show-jumping over deckchairs.

Carrie Jones

Everything I did with her seemed 'grown up', and she herself cultivated an airily sophisticated persona (though this was somewhat undermined by her great love of *Bunty* comic).

Caroline had an amazing belief in the rightness and superiority of everything she and her family did. This absolute confidence impressed me hugely and I was forever trying to figure out how she had banished the doubt and wariness about everything that so undermined my belief in myself.

In Caroline's life, objects seemed to give her a sense both of *being* in the world and of being *right* with the world: she always gave things their precise name which both amused me and (if I was feeling sorry for myself) made *my* object-lacking life seem the poorer. Her most precious belongings were things I had barely heard of and she made them seem impossibly glamorous. She had a red-leather 'vanity case' which she kept on the mirrored 'vanity unit' in her bedroom, and a leatherette 'pouffe' on which to sit before it. Ideally she would also attach a brand name to her possessions as well, lending them further cachet. The vanity case was Samsonite; the family record player was Grundig; they drank Mateus Rosé wine with their evening meal; their car was a Citroën Dyane – all these names stand out in my memory, because Caroline was constantly reciting her brand-name mantras.

In truth, not everything she had was absolutely top-notch, but the faith she had in her family's peerless excellence gave all her possessions a gloss that could not be tarnished. Caroline's mother regularly used to travel quite far to a factory shop, bringing back for her daughter bizarre items of clothing which no teenager of the time would have wanted to wear: a brown nylon blouse with orange polka-dots, tweed skirts, a tank-top with little appliqué cherries, and ribbed polo-necked sweaters in unappealing colours. But the way Caroline lovingly pronounced the factory's rag-trade name, you'd have thought she was dressed head-to-toe in Milan couture.

Caroline had two sisters and their house was like a sexless harem. Upstairs, their small bedrooms lined up along a narrow corridor. I used to find it quite frightening to walk the length of this landing, not knowing whether it was acceptable to look into the open doors of the rooms, perhaps to see one of the sisters doing serious womanly things. It was truly *Bunty* come to life and very alien to me. In fact I often had dreams that were almost nightmares about a house like Caroline's – or was it a girls' school? – with room upon room of knowing, powerful girls.

Fred Astaire was Caroline's pin-up because he looked like her Daddy. There was an Astaire movie on TV nearly every Sunday afternoon and the girls would sit in a line in their parents' bed gazing at the high-stepping Daddy *doppelganger*. (I couldn't bring myself to climb into the bed myself, it seemed far too intimate, so I would sit on the floor.) Caroline worshipped Daddy, kissing him on the top of his bald head and flirting with him in a way that made me feel uncomfortable. She flirted with *my* dad too, and that was even worse. *He* loved it when she posed for a photograph with his pipe in her mouth and giggled at him with a special liquid gurgle in her throat.

One summer Caroline and I went up to the Edinburgh Festival for a few days and at the very last minute my parents decided to take us up there in the car. I think they thought it would be possible to drive there and back in a day, but it was a much longer journey than they had imagined, so when we arrived at our B & B, they decided to spend the night and return home the next morning. That was grand, said the landlady, but we would have to make do with all sharing the one room. With everything arranged, and only me apparently with any misgivings, which I hid, we walked into the city to find cheap food and then went to the pictures – the film was *Fame*, I remember. Then it was back to our lodgings and the unspeakable darkness of my parents and me and my precocious friend all undressing and bedding down in the same room. And of course my mum and dad, not having expected to stay the night, had no nightclothes, no toothbrushes, nothing to normalise the situation. I didn't sleep. Sleep would have been deliverance, but I had to lie awake and listen to my father snoring and my sexy little friend giggling each time he groaned and sighed.

Where did Caroline learn her flirting skills? She was a nice girl from a very nice family, but she knew instinctively how to torture her admirers. She adored the film *Grease*, and I can no longer see the clip where Olivia Newton-John and John Travolta sing 'You're The One That I Want' without superimposing Caroline's face on the Neutron-Bomb's – she was that character made flesh-and-blood, the Good Girl with a poodle perm who beckons her man with a perfectly manicured finger, then crushes him under her stiletto heel.

When it came to mind games, Caroline could have had a great career as an interrogator in the Lubianka. I admired her skill – the way she gaily rejected her suitors whilst at the same time attaching them to her by an unbreakable silken thread – but I was simply too gauche to understand how she did it. And since the boys she toyed with were usually the same boys I had crushes on, I felt pity for them and, inevitably, resentment at the way I had been so neatly excised from the picture. I can remember her busily planning which route to take home from school one day in order to maximise the chances of 'bumping into' a key boy. Of course we *did* meet the boy, but she stonily ignored him. She got another boy who was crazy about her to give her his ratty homemade football scarf to wear as a token, then only wore it for a couple of days before nonchalantly handing it over to *me*. I adored this boy at the time, but, needless to say, couldn't be seen wearing the beloved scarf he had given to Caroline, so I was forced to hide it in my bedroom drawer and caress it in secret. As soon as she had got her hands on the woollen love trophy, Caroline had washed it (with superior Dreft soapflakes) so that it became strongly perfumed with the wholesome smell of Caroline's mother's laundry room. Perhaps that made it a Caroline token.

With her vanity case and vanity unit, Caroline was well-equipped to pay heed to her personal appearance, which she did with astonishing dedication. She worshipped at her mirror with its three lightbulbs illuminating her taut cheekbones and over-plucked eyebrows. Caroline had 'problem hair' – it was thin and greasy. Her diligent research into suitable brands of shampoo and conditioner (she favoured Linco beer shampoo for its raffishly adult overtones) had not solved the problem, but then Caroline got a perm. This was the making of her. Soft wavelets of honey-coloured hair lapped at her face and the effect, combined with candy-coloured blusher and a thick varnishing of lip gloss, was devastating. Boys were powerless to resist. Unfortunately, inside the delicate structures of her hair the perm was struggling to be permanent and the do soon began to look limp and sad. Another perm was the only solution, then another and another. One day the hairdresser refused to apply any more lotion, for fear that Caroline's hair would simply disintegrate, so that was the end of the perm era.

I was the plain sidekick to her cute juvenile lead, so it was only right that she should be prettier than me. And thinner, and curvier, and more perfumed. And her feet were neater. In fact my feet were huge and hers were verging on the trotter-like. Once, while we were getting changed after PE, Caroline suddenly placed her tiny little version of the latest shoe-fashion *right inside* my Desperate Dan version of the same shoe. The image of Caroline's shoe inside my shoe and her standing back to invite all the other girls in the locker room to come and mock the monster with the size 8s is still vivid.

My feet seemed to grow so fast that I barely had time to feel a momentary pleasure in some new fashion footwear my mum had bought me before I saw the first buckling of the cheap leather on the toecaps as my hateful big toes, like enemy sappers, began to tunnel towards the light. When my left foot (a good half size bigger than the right) came bursting through a pair of very recently bought shiny black shoes, I tried to disguise the hole with Elastoplast blackened with shoe polish but it was hopeless. Its flimsy defences were no match for my jutting toe, and the plaster flapped off almost immediately. (I had holes in most of my socks too, just like Nellie in 'On Mother Kelly's Doorstep', a song that my other granny, my father's mother, loved to bang out on the piano: 'Hole in her frock, Hole in her shoe, Hole in her stocking, Where her toe peeps through, But Nellie was the smartest down our alley…')

With Caroline G not only undermining my frail self-confidence with her innate physical superiority, but actually going out of her way to point up nature's unkindness, one might wonder why I was so loyal, so devotedly attached to her. I think it was because she would have me. In truth, I was in much the same position as her would-be boyfriends, but I was *inside* the charmed circle of her life. Maybe she played the same mind games with me that she played with them, but it was *me* who got to duet Rod

Stewart's 'Sailing' on the piano with her, *me* who got to lie on the floor sharing the headphones with her while we tried to work out the lyrics to 'Bohemian Rhapsody', *me* who got to look through her Fred Astaire part-work in its special ring-binder.

And it was me who got to kiss her.

Caroline and I got a regular babysitting job for a divorcee who, perhaps groping towards romance, had joined a choir. Every Tuesday we would spend the evening in her house. The child sleeping upstairs might as well not have been there. The drama was all ours. Being in that house was like being in another world; things could happen there which would never be referred to in the 'normal' world. Everything about our sessions was strangely ritualised. First of all we would cook Chef's Square-Shaped Soup, which we brought with us – either pea and ham or mushroom flavour – and eat it with toast in front of the television. Then we would lie on the sitting-room floor and 'practise kissing' for when we had boyfriends. I can remember the strong smell of the soup and how we pushed the heavy sofa back from the fire so that there was enough room for us to lie flat. Neither of us took the lead: I think it needed to seem wholly mutual. We rolled over and over, mimicking the wrestling match of 'real' kissing, the violence underlying sex as we were coming to perceive it. Giggling was out of the question. We maintained absolute seriousness, the kind of tuned-out dignity that characterises the gestures of a masque or ritual.

That this actually happened is hard to believe now. It's the only ostensibly 'lesbian' thing I have ever done. (There was a definite 'moment' years later, when I was lying in long grass in Kew Gardens with a friend from college. Overhead, huge slow planes were sinking down to land at Heathrow like massive phalluses. My friend picked up two beautiful, overripe peaches, and held them in front of her breasts, caressing them.) But, in fact, kissing Caroline had absolutely no lesbian overtones for me, it had no erotic content at all. I really believed I was practising my technique. (Yet how disingenuous that sounds. Perhaps I can only contemplate my transgressive teenage self by denying that there was any pleasure.) It can only have happened a few times and I had soon put it completely out of my mind. But I'm sure it was the reason Caroline started to avoid me after I went to college, once even lowering her umbrella over her eyes when we crossed paths one rainy day. All through the year after school, which we had both taken off, we wrote each other jolly, keep-your-pecker-up letters, but then Caroline got quite heavily involved in a religious group. I suspect it was their highly moralistic stance which recast her memory of our childish kisses in a more sordid light and made her feel retrospectively 'dirty'. All her sisters became caught up in the same group and once, when one of them visited me briefly in Cambridge, I saw at first-hand how their sense of fun had been choked by a doctrine of disapproval. I had rooms on the ground-floor of the college court, looking out onto a big lawn where, on this day, a garden party was taking place. As Caroline's sister and I stood watching the party, a boy ran up to a girl and slid an ice-cube down the back of her dress. There was much squealing and over-excited mock-wrestling. The sister's face contorted with distaste and she muttered, 'How disgusting!'

About fifteen years after we left school somebody organised a school reunion in a hotel a few miles from our home town. I should have known better than to go. I hadn't seen or spoken to Caroline G for most of those years. She was there, with a fresh silky perm, high colour on her cheeks and a pastel-coloured clutch bag under her arm. As we exchanged banal small talk,

I became fixated on the clutch bag and it began to seem ludicrous, to encapsulate all the glammed-up, high-heeled emptyheadedness of my ex-best friend. Without saying goodbye to anyone, I cadged a lift back to town with our old headmaster who had been invited to give a little opening speech and was now escaping, as was I.

Caroline was my 'best friend' yet I both idolised and quite intensely disliked her. We were ill-matched in almost every way, and yet our closeness was universally acknowledged and deferred to. No one ever challenged me for Caroline's hand. To have had such a best friend and then to lose her, quietly, without sparks or declarations or any sort of falling out, seems strange. But now when I am back at home for Christmas I dread seeing her much more than I fear bumping into an old boyfriend. I don't ever want to have to look into her eyes and see the complete absence of the connection that was once there.

Chapter 6

FASCIST REGIME

Went to Leeds for a 7th Form French conference. The lecture on L'Etranger *was really good. Best thing was we went into this Leftist political book/newspaper/badge shop. Would've loved to browse and buy loads of propaganda, but only dared buy a* Temporary Hoarding *and a 'Nazis No Fun' badge to replace my Anti-Nazi League badge which got pogoed off at the TRB concert.*

Diary entry, April 3 1979 (age 16)

BY 1978 my secret passion for punk music was verging on obsession. I would go to bed at ten o'clock every night, just as the John Peel show started. Night after night, my bedroom was a mad scientist's dream of sensory over-stimulation and discomfort. To listen to the radio in bed I had to wear headphones. To do this I had to lie on my stomach with my head held stiffly at a precise angle: any further left and the left-hand earpiece would bore into my skull; any further right and I would suffocate. I couldn't lie on my back as then I wouldn't have been able to operate the piano-key controls of the coffee-table-sized 'music centre' which had been my reward for doing well in my O-levels (and which was perhaps also an admission of defeat by my dad in his war against pop music). With my hand stretched out from under the covers into the freezing room and my fingers resting on the pause button, I could instantly start the tape recorder when a song I liked came on.

After about half an hour I would become drowsy. Then I

would fall into semi-sleep, only to be wrenched out of it by the neurotic pulsing of a Throbbing Gristle track. Down, down again... then, whack, an adrenalin shot of the Fall straight into the cerebral cortex. Finally I would fall asleep, my bloodless fingers just managing to throw the giant on/off switch before I lost consciousness.

There was another nightly assault on my brain. Before he went to bed, my father would switch on the outside light and go up the back garden to fetch Coalite to keep the Parkray stove in the Orange Room going through the night. A dazzling rhomboid of light would then be thrown into my room, waking me up. Against this warped screen a sinister cartoon of my dad, stretched into a German Expressionist monster, the coal scuttle a hideous truncheon in his hand, would stalk up the wall, his footsteps surreally echoing outside. I felt his savage pleasure as he drove the scuttle into the pile of Coalite — my stomach would cramp up every night at the sharp bark it made. Then, a little while later, he would come upstairs and, on his way to bed, either come right into my room and stand by my bed, or stand in the doorway, for what seemed an age. I felt his regret for the awkwardness that stopped us from communicating, and I flattened myself under the covers and tried to melt into the mattress.

On 28 March 1979, a Wednesday night with school the next day, my secret love of punk drove me to commit the most rebellious act of my teenage years. Telling my mum and dad that I was going to a classical orchestra concert in the neighbouring town, I went to see the Tom Robinson Band playing around fifty miles away. A strange white-haired boy in my class had a car, a dreadful old thing but tolerable if it meant I could get to see my heroes. I knew Brian Smedley was strange because he was going out with Karen Holmes and she had told me many times of her struggle to concoct meals that he would eat. Even though both parties still lived with their mums and dads, Karen liked to provide solid meals for her boyfriends. She also knitted them sweaters and went round the shops with them on a Saturday afternoon in an effort to create an aura of domestic happiness. But Brian Smedley would not be a meat-and-two-veg man, not even for Karen. He liked hard-boiled eggs, but had a horror of tomatoes; he would eat her sturdy cheese scones, but nothing with raisins. He was awkward, but she seemed to love him the more for that.

Obviously Karen could not sanction my travelling to see the TRB with Brian unaccompanied, so she came too, even though *her* musical passion was Dean Friedman. My chaperone was Caroline G.

Brian's car had a serious fault: every so often the engine would die and Brian would have to get out, lift the bonnet and tap some valve which fed petrol into the carburettor and then it would go again – for a brief stretch. On this particular night it was raining the sort of rain you only usually get in Hollywood with the aid of powerful hoses. Four times Brian had to unfold his scrawny form from behind the wheel of the car and tinker with the dodgy valve. I remember sitting in the back of the car with Caroline, trying not to breathe in the smell of Brian's wet donkey jacket and feeling increasingly nervous about having lied to my parents.

We eventually arrived at the 'gig'. (I always felt tremendously self-conscious about saying the word 'gig', still do; I can't even write it without distancing myself from it with inverted commas.) The evening's entertainment was interminably drawn out, with hour-long gaps after each of the instantly forgettable support bands. Standing in the crush during the dull interludes, I got talking to a boy called Col. He spoke with the strong local accent and had straight dark hair that fell diagonally across his forehead, rather like Hitler's. He was the same height and age as me and very friendly, but in an offhand way, as though he would have been exactly the same regardless of who he had found standing next to him. He was very excited about the bands and identified strongly with the performers, straining to connect with them through the intensity of his gaze, his jerky dancing mirroring theirs. In the breaks between bands, *he* could be the star attraction – and I was an attentive audience of one. In my diary I wrote that he 'kissed my finger where I'd gouged a hole in it doing up my jeans when they were very tight'. A couple of days previously I had won a copy of Blondie's new album, *Parallel Lines*, by writing a review of a TRB record for our local paper. I liked having my finger kissed so much that when Col declared a liking for Blondie, I offered to send him the album. I was quite taken with him. In the context of the dark, noisy dancehall he had real bad-boy glamour, mostly because of his ugly accent. I was a frightful snob about accents.

It was half-past one in the morning before we set off to return home. The rain was still pounding down but Brian seemed to have given the petrol valve a definitive nudge and we were making good progress. I was staring into the darkness, imagining meeting Col again so that he could kiss my finger for hours on end and hoping my parents weren't waiting up for me, when the blue flashing light of a police van and a policeman flagging us down with a torch broke my introspection. We were the four most innocent teenagers in Britain, but that didn't stop us being terrified of instant strip-searches and imprisonment without trial. This was the era of the SUS laws and we had just spent an evening being exposed to high-volume, sustained paranoia about the 'pigs' and the evil 'Fascist State'.

Brian nervously rolled down his window.

'Evening, sir. I'm afraid the motorway is flooded by three feet of water and you'll have to turn off. You should be all right once you're off here. Have a safe journey.'

It was hardly Blackshirt behaviour. So much for the Fascist State. We drove off the motorway and found the right direction for home. The place-names were starting to be familiar from Saturday afternoon outings with my dad and my granny (her hobby was comparing the price of a pound of bacon at different butchers throughout the north-east), when my semi-sleep was disturbed by the sound of water sluicing up the flanks of the car. The engine struggled against a mass of liquid. This road was flooded too.

We managed to push through the flood and park outside a small hotel up ahead. In the foyer a log fire was burning and the manager was kind enough to let us sit in its warmth until daybreak. It was a real adventure with that rare feeling of being outside time and place. There was a jolly frontier spirit, but I couldn't join in with it because I was frantic about having lied to my parents about where I'd gone. I decided to ring them and come clean. Standing with my head under the hairdryer-like hood of the public phone by the toilets, I let the phone ring and ring and ring. There was no answer. Were they out combing the fields and ditches, looking for me? Had the police been brought in?

I spent the rest of the night in terrible agitation. I tried ringing again, several times, but there was never any answer. My agitation wasn't quite so terrible as to prevent me from sticking

Anti-Nazi League stickers in the women's lavatories with Caroline (even though there weren't many Nazis in rural Yorkshire), but it was with ghastly trepidation that I climbed back into Brian's car to finish our journey home, once daylight had returned and the rain had stopped.

They dropped me off outside my house and I went inside. It was around seven o'clock. There were no police anoraks hung over the banisters, no crackle of walky-talkies, no earnest WPC making my weeping mother another cup of tea. Only silence. I went upstairs and put my head round my parents' bedroom door. Two separate lumps doming the covers in the grey light, just the same as usual. I went into my own bedroom and crawled beneath the sheets. Was it possible that I had got away with it? That they had *not* been up all night desperately searching for me? I was torn between relief that my lie had gone undiscovered, and dismay that they didn't seem to care that I had been out all night. My carefully maintained image was that of a nice teenager who never put a foot wrong for fear of upsetting her parents. It was hard work keeping this up and it caused me a lot of anxiety if the mask slipped, as it had this night. But if they didn't care, then what was the point of all my hang-ups?

Perhaps I obsessively kept what I thought of as my *real self* secret because secrecy enhanced everything, made it seem more important, more special (my equivalent of Caroline G's brand-names). And secret things were protected things; no one could make fun of them or carelessly show up their true ordinariness or inferiority. In the absence of other children when I was small, I had always lived in my imagination and been happy there. As I grew older, nothing happened to alter my belief that secret meant precious.

* * * *

The day after the concert I sent the Blondie album to Col. Even as I was wrapping it up, I knew that Col was 'unsuitable' – that he was a bit thick and a bit 'common' – but the appeal of secret communication with a boy I'd met at a secret punk concert was too great to ignore.

I've still got the letters Col wrote me over the course of the next few months. No one ever knew about the correspondence: thanks to my hovering behind the net curtains each morning, I was able to intercept every single letter as it came through the door. They are the least romantic letters it is possible to imagine – Col did dull with consummate skill – and it's obvious he wasn't the least bit interested in me. True, he did send me a cardboard bowtie given out at a gig by his favourite band, the Rezillos, but was careful to let me know he had two, in case I should be stupid enough to think any kind of sacrifice was involved.

He promised to send me a tape of cool music ('Tubeway Army, Devo, Rezillos, B52s, X-Ray Spex...') as well as every variation of the '...Against the Nazis' badge, but nothing ever came. He was a master of the let-down. I don't really know why he bothered to keep writing back, except that the idea of 'penfriends' still had real currency in those pre-chatroom, pre-emailing, pre-texting days. Also, we were at that age of pop-obsession when it seems important to *tell* other people what you like, in order to validate your choices.

Since Col, I've had other reluctant boyfriends, who've even slept with me once or twice in spite of not really liking me very much at all. Now I would recognise that in-spite-of-themselves regret at not having been able to resist an invitation to get involved when really they knew they didn't want to and I would graciously help them off the hook, but with Col I just kept on trying to reel him in.

One day we planned to meet up in a town halfway between our homes. Yet again, this involved subterfuge on my part, probably quite unnecessarily: I told my mother I was going shopping with Caroline. I had to take a bus and a train to get there, and for two hours I sat on a bench at the appointed meeting place, waiting for Col to turn up. He didn't. The next day a brief letter arrived: he had been 'having trouble with wisdom teeth, dentist doped me up to the eyeballs...Various people tried to phone but with no success...' Amazing how unreliable the phone system could be in the late Seventies. It would have to be a short note, he wrote, as 'my mouth is swelling up again'. I should surely have been suspicious, but no, in my diary, it is all cooing over 'poor darling Col'. He was really little more than an excuse for me to write such things; the reality was so distant from my rosy interpretation of it.

A few months later, just before I went to France to au pair, after a silence from him of a few weeks, I wrote in my diary: *'I made a last attempt, a reckless heartfelt plea. It worked. He wrote this morning. But the reason why he hadn't written before was awful – he had been laid up in hospital after being in a car crash. Is there no end to his bad luck?'* Oh *really*, I want to slap my teenage self! Reading his pathos-drenched letter now, it's *so* obvious that he was on a glorious roll, making up any old tripe to get this tedious posh bird off his back. It is wonderful Billy Liar stuff: *'A Cortina appeared out of a side street and smashed into the back of our car. Everybody was shaken and received minor injuries such as broken legs, ribs, teeth, and in my case a broken arm and also broken ribs ... As I lay in hospital, unable to write and sick of the sight of parents bringing endless bunches of grapes which I can't stand, I often tried to send you messages by E.S.P... I even asked Si to write to you but he couldn't get a verbal message right... after eight weeks I deserved a discharge...'* Eight weeks in hospital for a broken arm and ribs – no wonder the Health Service was in tatters. But even though I had suffered a broken arm myself and it had received no more attention than an x-ray snap by a surly radiographer who was working to rule, a quick plaster cast and home, I refused to smell a rat.

Perhaps I preferred my boyfriends far away and entirely unreliable as they were less likely to enter my 'real life' and cause me embarrassment in front of my mum and dad. Col was virtually fictional. 'Loving' him was just like 'loving' David Cassidy or Tom Robinson except that instead of a cheap fanclub newsletter I got letters on cheap blue writing paper. It didn't matter that the letters were stupid and boring; they were signs of my *connection* to a boy. The connection made me feel special and – even better – I didn't have to grapple with any problematic flesh.

Mess with flesh and you're in trouble.

Chapter 7

ALLONS, ENFANTS DE LA PATRIE

It could be worse – I could be here for ever, or in prison, or in a war, or with a dreadful illness. I am well off compared to millions of other people. The Cambodians, for example, or those American hostages in Iran ... I am going down to iron now and listen to the Boomtown Rats.

Diary entry, 28 November 1979 (age 17)

MY 'gap' year after school as an au pair girl for an uptight French family passed excruciatingly slowly.

I don't remember whose idea it was for me to spend the year before university in France. My parents never sat me down to discuss the choices open to me; no other ideas had been bandied about and then rejected. As far as I knew, no one took any particularly vigorous action on my behalf, but before the summer was out I was installed *chez* the Berthauds. I occupied their attic, a room whose ceiling sloped so exaggeratedly that the only place where I could stand fully upright was in the dormer window. The *salon* had a precious parquet floor that no one was allowed to walk on; instead you had to stand on feet-shaped cut-outs of carpet and glide across – the sight of M. Berthaud, tall and slightly pigeon-chested, skating across the parquet fatally undermined my respect for him. Nestled in the gloom at the far end of the room was an ornate settee, upholstered with fauxleopardskin plush and so tightly stuffed that when three people sat on it (as, alas, I would quite often have to with Monsieur et

Madame) the middle sitter would be jauntily upright, whilst the two on either side would be pointing up into opposite corners of the room, rather like the small bunches of very expensive and very carefully arranged lilies which M. Berthaud would bring home for Mme. Berthaud on special occasions. Even though I had the whole of Paris to explore in my free time, I still felt as though I was a prisoner in a particularly twee jail. I was just too big for that primped and prissy little suburban house.

As for looking after the *enfants* Berthaud, I was seriously out of my depth. Not only was I an only child, I had had virtually no social contact with any other children at all throughout my entire life, apart from at school. In fact I was afraid of children. Isabelle and Olivier were terrifying.

At eight, Olivier was a veteran in the war of attrition against au pair girls. He had yellow teeth with serrated edges, like brass knives, and most of the time they were bared, either in manic laughter or rage. If he didn't want to do his homework or go to bed, he would lie stretched out on the sitting-room parquet, gripping the spindly leg of the Louis Quatorze-style television stand (the house was full of such kitsch anachronisms), which was already close to collapse from previous incidents. Isabelle, four, was prone to mentioning a pain in some part of her body or other, which, if I responded favourably (that is, showed any concern), soon developed into a full-scale *crise*.

At least I had my programme of Saturday outings. Once I had left M. et Mme. Berthaud nervously eyeing their children I would catch the train into Paris, each time heading for a different part of the city and then walking up and down the streets and boulevards so that I could colour them in on my map when I got home. Perhaps it was a little lacking in spontaneity, but I did get to know Paris very well, even if the delights of Père Lachaise cemetery and the Pompidou Centre, the Marais and the Latin Quarter were somewhat dampened by regular incidents with the city's men. A good number of these managed to rub their crotches against me in the Metro or reach up to a high shelf from behind me in bookshops (same result) or scrutinise gallery paintings at close quarters (my quarters) — same result. I was constantly on my guard for bulging eyeballs and bulging trousers. The strap of my satchel bag firmly crossing my chest like an all-purpose chastity belt, I marched the streets with a don't-touch-me stiffness to my stride, eyes narrowed, scanning ahead for would-be gropers. With this attitude, it was no wonder I didn't stumble across a nice boyfriend. What a wasted opportunity! Now it's painfully easy to imagine the dreamy afternoons I could have spent caressing some Jean-Paul Belmondo lookalike, or kicking leaves in the Jardin du Luxembourg with my very own Alain Delon, but I was Mlle Uptight.

You might think that leaving home at seventeen to come to Paris would be wildly romantic — the long-awaited freedom from the closed-circuit surveillance of my extended family. But I think this inrush of freedom was too great for me. I went into shock, and only coped by imposing my own even more suffocating regime. After months of lonely pavement-pounding and having nothing more exciting in my bedroom than the odd moth, I began, eventually, to thaw out into fantasies. I remember sitting on my bed one afternoon, dressed up in an antique white-lace camisole and petticoat. I was imagining myself at college, how I would be so confident there, ready for adventure. I cupped my breasts and looked at myself in the mirror. I wondered who would be there with me, validating me with their gaze. Suddenly I heard the front door open and close, and M. Berthaud was hallooing stiffly up the stairs. Unheard of for Monsieur B to come home in the middle of the afternoon! It was as if he had been drawn by the sexual current that had finally escaped from my heavily insulated core. But in reality there was no frisson of excitement. M. Berthaud's dusty features and obsession with protocol made him sexually non-existent – he would grow pale with embarrassment if I ever accidentally addressed him as *tu*. I threw on my jeans and T-shirt and went downstairs to let him practise his English on me – he had told me only to speak to him in English when Madame was not there. The implication was that she would be very threatened if we spoke incomprehensibly in front of her. He specially enjoyed talking about food and would make me repeat 'shepherd's pie' or 'yoghurt', 'sausages' or 'chocolate sponge' over and over again while he tried to catch the precise way of saying them. 'Lemon meringue pie, lemon meringue pie, spotted dick, spotted dick, spotted dick'.

Surely there was someone…? At last, I managed to contrive a half-hearted crush on Nicolas Dupuy, the ascetic conductor of the *Harmonie Municipale*, the town wind band which I'd joined in order to have an excuse to leave the house in the evenings. At least he had the glamour of authority. He must have been in his twenties, rather effete and formal, with a fleshless face and wire-rimmed glasses. He always wore a navy-blue blazer with gilt buttons and wide-legged pale silvery-grey trousers.

Smiles, attentiveness, lingering for after-rehearsal chats – hardly the behaviour of an obsessive maniac. But for a long time Nicolas seemed to find my attentions oppressive. The band was an official offshoot of the municipality, so in a sense we were all *fonctionnaires* – perhaps for that reason he felt it wasn't quite *comme il faut*. And I wasn't even French. He hid behind a screen of formality; it seemed only a matter of time before he would be clicking his heels together and bowing when we met. But in the end my persistent appreciation of his jokes and my ploy of exaggerating how nervous I was about walking home after rehearsals through the ill-lit town centre paid off. He began to give me a lift home every week. We exchanged only the most correct *bisous* on each cheek on parting, but eventually I broke his resistance and he invited me on a date.

We met at the Parc Monceau on a cool Sunday afternoon in early Spring. Parc Monceau is where O's lover René takes her for a walk in the opening sentence of *The Story of O*, and it was beautiful — an acre of poised French formality. Unlike René, though, Nicolas had not arranged for a mysterious car to take me away to a chateau for initiation into sado-masochistic rites. No, after a polite stroll around the statues of Guy de Maupassant and Frederic Chopin, we visited the nearby Musée Nissim de Camondo, definitely the most obscure of all the obscure museums I ticked off during my year in France. It housed a severe collection of eighteenth-century furniture and ornaments to make a girl weep with boredom. When we emerged into the sunshine there was awkwardness. Nicolas was in civvies: his neatly pressed jeans and polo-neck jumper relieved him of the need to observe official propriety — but only to a degree. We moved in a controlled and dignified manner through the formal phases of our afternoon together until we had arrived at the end of the planned activity. We stood on the edge of scrubland, the neat beds and paths behind us, only the confusion of choice and possibilities before us. I could see the unease in Nicolas' pale eyes as he scanned this inner landscape, his reluctance to risk getting his shoes dusty, his reputation tarnished. He was even more awkward than me, I realised, and suffering agonies of uncertainty about what to do with me. Hold hands? Propose marriage? I decided to save him; I made up an excuse so that I wouldn't have to travel back to the suburbs with him, and escaped.

That afternoon was nearly the romantic peak of my year as an au pair.

Then, with just one week to go, I was invited out with some friends who had just taken their *baccalaureat*. A group of about eight of us went to a nightclub in the Latin Quarter called, wonderfully, the Whisky A Go Go. I can almost believe that it wasn't a real place at all but a devilish illusion conjured up out of my imagination, my idea of the perfect nightclub wherein all decadence, all lust would be unleashed to debauch me.

The others in the group were those typical middle-class French teenagers whose hard work at school and serious application to the task of absorbing French culture ensures that they become excellent citizens and get good jobs for life. Their complexions pimply and pale from the long months of revision for the *bac*, they sat smiling and sipping red wine. The music was very very loud, hammering your chest and atomising your inhibitions.

The club was full of young men with severe haircuts and one of these motioned me to dance. Pleased to be singled out, I danced. I bounced and skipped and spun – all the moves I had practised on the Berthauds' parquet floor (*without* the carpet feet-shapes! What a rebel!) whilst ironing Olivier's miniature shirts and listening to the Boomtown Rats, the only LP I had with me. The boy looked entranced. He yelled in my ear that his name was Alain. I yelled my name in his and he realised that I was *anglaise*. So much the better. I let the relentless music invade me and I became its puppet, holding Alain's gaze and grinning at him. I wasn't trying to bewitch him, but I felt I had to hold a really brilliant smile on Alain to signal to him my continuing and unwavering pleasure at his company, my gratitude at his having chosen *me*. My jaw began to ache from the smiling. It was as though I was focusing rays of light on him through the magnifying glass of my mouth – any longer and he might have burst into flames. We subsided against the wall and kissed, an almighty, disco-charged, sweat-drenched French slurp, as deep and wet as a well. The music and the heat and the other bodies packed us into an airless chamber of arousal. We sucked and chewed away at each other, trying to magic the grinding of our bodies into a merging of our flesh. I've no idea what the kids I'd come with thought: I never saw them again.

'*Less goh...*' Alain's command of English was clearly a source of great pride. He steered me towards the door, we collected our coats, and suddenly we were freed from the club's bacchanalian grip and out in the cool Paris night.

It was about two in the morning and the streets were emptying. Holding hands, we walked down towards the Seine. I wasn't nervous – this was 'romantic'. Alain tried to talk to me in English, but when he realised that my French was so fluent he gave up. He told me that he was a trainee pilot in the French air force (I don't think I had quite the required reaction of awed respect and admiration) and that he was in Paris, along with thousands of other soldiers and sailors and airmen for the Bastille Day parade down the Champs Elysées. That's why the club had been so full of neat-haired young men. And now, out of the nearly random coming together of one of those identikit young men and me, it seemed a grand passion had been born. But on what basis? His face had a slight thickness to the features, which, combined with the military crewcut, made him look like a throwback to the Forties. He seemed like an animated photograph, somehow. Now that I could see him properly, I didn't really fancy him, but I didn't want this thought to take hold in my mind: revulsion might follow all too quickly. I tried to block out the mental picture of us writhing and nearly coupling in the nightclub – I knew that I had made a choice of some sort in leaving the club with Alain but, at the same time, I opted not to admit to myself what that choice entailed. I went along with the unfolding drama, rather than putting a stop to it right away, because if I had, it would have seemed so *ungracious*. It was to be a very long time before I stopped being grateful for any man's interest in me; gratitude makes people submissive.

We came down to the embankment and started to walk along beside the grey river. As we passed under a bridge Alain stopped and pressed me against the arched wall. He kissed me urgently and started to undo my jeans. He put my hand on his trousers where an enormous erection pleaded for liberation. Swinging my hips to the side like a hula girl to free myself, I smiled in what I hoped was an alluring way and shook my head.

'Non, non, non.' I certainly didn't want to lose my virginity standing under a bridge; but I had aroused him to a point of keen expectation and now he was focused on achieving satisfaction. God, those *things*, what were they like? The last stiffy – the *only* stiffy – I had had actual hold of was Mark Sykes', and then only briefly. Just long enough to be awed by its ugliness, its unfleshliness, more like, say, an ergonomically designed garden implement, oh but hot and with a particular smell, not bad but fierce, the whole thing so very unignorable. Needing to be dealt with. Apart from Mark's there had occasionally been others, not unleashed but forceful nonetheless, locked inside trousers, accusing *me* of causing their discomfort, pointing a finger at *me* for getting them all razzled up and then denying them release. I had very recently been to see the film *Alien* and had been unable to block out the thought that the alien 'birth-pod' (if I'm

remembering rightly) was incredibly, indulgently penile, with its ridges and veins. It hadn't helped that there had been a man very obviously masturbating under a folded macintosh, just a couple of seats along from me. Now I could virtually see the ridges and veins of Alain's 'birth-pod' through its thick cotton sheathing. It *was* a kind of trophy for me, a reward for being fanciable (though maybe just for being female and there). I could exult in it, but I didn't desire it. I was still years away from feeling the pure urge to be filled. At the same time I felt that, having brought it forth, I couldn't just walk away from it. I owed it something. In fact, this was virtually all I felt – a sense of obligation, of the price to be paid for arousing a man.

I myself was not aroused, or not any more. Perhaps in the gyrating, sucking slick of bodies in the club I might have lost my head – *and* my 'maidenhead' – if we had stayed, although I don't think in those days people actually had sex on the dance floor, even in the most salacious Paris *boîtes*. But in the cold night air I was suddenly smilingly detached. I was still quite pleased with my lucky-dip French boy. I was still willing to flirt, but now I was on the defensive.

Benny Hill was big in France at that time, and perhaps Alain was a fan of Benny's speeded-up chase sequences with suspender-belted girls wagging their fingers at the naughty boy and wobbling away behind trees and round park benches. Now we performed our own comedy pursuit scene, with me trying to remain on the right side of chastity whilst doing my best to keep Alain sweet with my coquettishness. He just wanted to get inside my pants. I didn't feel physically threatened, but I had never before been under this sort of sustained pressure to deliver myself up for deflowering. Alain said we could go to a hotel. I knew that I was not going to yield. I was back in the mindset of a sensible girl and I wasn't about to 'do something stupid'. I was starting to get blisters.

The chase began to exhaust us. I was getting irritated by Alain's very French persistence, and he was becoming *un tout petit peu* truculent as well. Dawn had broken and the traffic was building up for another day. The Metro was running again, and I said that I was going home. Alain said that he would come too. Perhaps he thought that I would finally succumb under the satin coverlet in M. Berthaud's attic! But that, of course, was unthinkable. I had never brought anyone into that house, let alone a rampant male hell-bent on fornication.

Alain came with me right to the wrought-iron garden gate. He still had a squint of hope in his eye as I kissed him goodbye and prayed that neither Monsieur nor Madame was looking out of the window.

I had told Alain that I was going back to England at the end of the week and now he asked me to scribble my address on a piece of paper so that he could write to me. He seemed very down now, resentful that I had resisted his passion. I didn't look back as I walked up the path and into the house. I went to bed and slept for as long as I could until Olivier and Isabelle came and woke me up.

The next day was the 14th of July and I watched the Bastille Day parade on television. I didn't catch sight of Alain among the thousands of military men clipping down the Champs Elysées. I was embarrassed to think of how the music and the dark heat of the Whisky A Go Go had seduced me and brought me so close to 'ruin' (I had read far too many melodramatic French novels over the past twelve months). But had I not clung to my innocence? Was I not still *viérge*? Virtue had won the day. Anyway, I was going home in a couple of days, so what did it matter?

Cutting Up Playgirl

My father came to collect me. Filthy and tired from the journey, and having been dreadfully lost in the ring-road system, he sat on the Berthauds' leopardskin sofa looking like a despairing bear crammed into a gilded cage. The next morning we loaded up the car with all the plates I had not been able to resist buying in the bargain basements at Printemps and Galeries Lafayette. So many plates! – but all absolutely necessary for the grand life I imagined I was going to have at Cambridge. Oh the tea parties I would have! The plates I would fill with Chelsea buns at my lovely tea parties!

Goodbye France! *Adieu*, not *au revoir*. Plates rattling, we set off home and I couldn't wait to be there. I was so glad it was over. As far as I was concerned, I had done my time, stuck it out; now I was paroled and just waiting for Cambridge to start. Nothing much had changed at home: it was all still rather mutedly miserable. But it was the muted misery of my own home, not the Berthauds' muted misery, and that had to be good. Like mustard, give me English muted misery over French any day! I quickly fell back into the old summer routines of reading books on the brown corduroy mattress in the back garden, picking the single fruit that ripened each day in the poisoned-looking remains of our old strawberry bed, playing draughts with my dad over a cheese-and-onion pasty from the butcher's in the marketplace every lunchtime.

About ten days after I had come home, easily long enough for everything to seem quite normal again, I was just picking up the last greasy crumbs of that day's pasty from my plate when the doorbell rang. There were the usual fearful glances at each other: no one was expected. My mother hurriedly started to put a bit of lipstick on. My dad set off down the long passage to the front door. I was clearing away the plates – it was shameful to be discovered eating cheese-and-onion pasties by an unexpected caller – when I heard my dad calling me. His voice had that particular north-east twang that you only heard at times of stress.

'Carrie, military gentleman for you…'

My stomach heaved. The pasty made a swift bid to return to daylight. Swallowing hard, I walked down the dim hall to the blinding rectangle of the open front door. There, in full blue-serge uniform, stood Alain, a huge canvas bag at his feet.

'*Salut*, Carrie.'

This was catastrophe. It was one thing to snog an unknown French soldier in a Paris nightclub and then spend half the night keeping him out of my knickers in the murky shadows under bridges, but I had managed to *contain* that, to get through it unscathed. It was supposed to be *over. Discreetly* over. Now, like a mythological beast in a Hollywood epic, which, beheaded, springs back to life with not one but two heads, the dirty little secret of my night with Alain had burst through the *cordon sanitaire* I'd thrown around it and was writhing around, spewing filth and shame. My parents would think I had spent my entire year in France screwing soldiers. I was pole-axed.

'What are you doing here?'

Alain said he had flown a French air force plane to RAF Brize Norton and then hitchhiked from there. With hindsight, it seems very unlikely that he actually piloted a plane, but perhaps he was able to cadge a lift somehow. Perhaps he was AWOL? Who knows? Now he was expecting to be welcomed with open arms and invited to stay at our house. No way! I felt outraged that he had come, unannounced, and blown my maidenly cover. I was *so* angry with him. (I've just been poring over Alain's letters, which I was never able to decipher and which I still find almost impossible to read. There's one dated July 17th, so only three days after Bastille Day, and I can make out the words *'Demain la Manche'* – 'tomorrow the Channel' – so perhaps he *did* write to say he was coming, but I hadn't received that letter by the time he turned up.) The intensity of my embarrassment combined with the shock of his appearance made me highly unpredictable.

I allowed Alain into the house, just as far as the cold front room, and then I left him to go and face my parents. In the kitchen there was a current of excitement, not to say hilarity. My mum was making Alain his first cup of tea and getting out the Kitkats. My dad seemed rather impressed.

'Who's this fellow, then?'

I could hardly bring myself to answer. Anyway, what was the answer? 'He's just ... he's just somebody I met. Nobody special...'

'Seems like a nice enough bloke. What's his name?'

'Alain.' I hated saying his name with its horrible mush of French sounds underlining the wrongness of his presence here, now. 'I'll get rid of him.'

'Oh, no need for that...' I heard my dad saying as I went back down the passage to the front room.

'You can't stay here. Sorry. I'm going away.' This was nearly true. I'd been talking about going to Cambridge for a few days with Caroline G, for the music festival. Nothing would stop me now. I let Alain drink his tea and then I made him leave. His face was clouded with disappointment as I shut the door on him, but that evening he came back, his lusts renewed, fresh vigour in his limbs. He had pitched his Air-Force-issue tent down by the river with the intention of continuing his campaign on my virginity. In the meantime I had fixed up my escape with Caroline G and we were going to get the train to Cambridge the next day. I'd booked a guest room at my college. Perhaps knowing that I was going to get away made me relax my guard: I agreed to go for a walk with Alain.

It was the night of the bridges all over again, only worse. This time we went along our road, past the bench where I had sat with Mark, and over the stile into the woods. In among the trees the twilight deepened and Alain was more determined than ever that I should yield to him. Once again, typically, I was happy to go so far, but then no further. Instead of simply having nothing to do with him, I made the mistake of trying to appease him by going a little way. Of course that just maddened him. As the smooth trunks of the saplings around us glowed white in the darkness, Alain's erection was presented to me in supplication. It was lucky I could barely see it as I would probably have been terrified. How far would be too far? He'd come such a long way, it seemed only fair to go a teensy bit further. Maybe it would make him feel better...

I knew NOTHING about men.

We rolled about on the sloping, dusty earth under the trees. Alain was pleading, almost weeping with frustration. I kissed him and patted vaguely at his cock with my hand as if to say, yes, there there, I know. Just to acknowledge it, really. Not to would have seemed rude. Alain manoeuvred it between my legs and began to rock on top of me, moaning. Swiftly checking my sensible girl's mental handbook of pregnancy risks, I decided that this was not 'doing something stupid' and I allowed him to heave himself about on top of me until he came all over my thighs. There, surely he'd be happy now? Wiping myself down with dock leaves, I felt that honour had been done and in a satisfactorily practical way. What more did he want, coming here uninvited? – and anyway I fancied him even less now.

At that moment, I weighed up the pros and cons of the *real man* — Alain with his probing hands and fountaining penis — versus the *cardboard man* — stand-in lovers such as pen-pal Col, crush-object Jamie, pop-star Tom (*gay!* — in those days he was anyway) — and came to the conclusion that the cardboard versions were a lot less trouble, much more amenable, and certainly not so leaky. I had wanted a boyfriend, had longed for one, just like any teenager, but I had not bargained on the real thing being so *difficult.*

I sent Alain on down through the woods as the path led straight to the river. Then I ran home and spent the rest of the evening watching television with my mum and dad as if nothing had happened. They were obviously intensely curious about Alain but they knew better than to quiz me about him.

If they had, I would not have been able to tell them. The breath for telling them was blocked in my throat. My growing up must be ruthlessly denied. I would rather be just a brain on a stick — sexless, genderless, safe. Was this my parents' doing or mine? To all appearances, there was nothing untoward about them. They didn't punish me for having contact with boys, they didn't try to prevent me from meeting boys; I'm sure they thought it was completely normal and would have taken it in their stride if I had had a string of boyfriends.

The thing was that they were very unhappy with each other, had been almost from the outset, but had found themselves married with a child and were, for whatever reasons, keeping the pretence going. The little family was forlorn, there was not enough love to go around, but the little girl was very loving and could love mummy and could love daddy. How hungrily they took her love, jealously watching to see if the other one got more than they did. She would go from one to the other, topping them up, keeping them happy, spinning plates.

Instead of a solid triangle, there were two separate couples, with me as both substitute wife and substitute husband. In the competition for my affections there were no holds barred: games were played, secrets were shared… (My dad and I had an almost continuous game of 'laggy-bat' for years – 'laggy-bat' was no-holds-barred tag, the name an insane, distorted version of 'tag you back' that we screamed as we lunged at each other; I also loved being tied up in a blanket by him and having to escape, Houdini-like. With my mum it was less physical: I was the recipient of everything she needed to unburden herself of – worries at work, exciting encounters, sadness and badness. I was the validator who made things real by hearing them.) But a sense of self-preservation must have prevailed, or else a sense of guilt. I did collude in the games, I did revel in the secrets I was privy to, but I must have known that I could not, should not be spouse to my parents. So my fitness for the role had to be obliterated by concealing or denying my sexuality. If I revealed myself to be sexually aware, knowledgeable, worse still sexually active, it would make my role in relation to each of my parents too explicit. I would be 'asking for it'. There might have been an element of Electra-like desire for my father – natural enough, perhaps – but at the same time that desire was profoundly taboo. Thus, my behaviour was perhaps both inhibited *and* over-sexualised – the more I became aware of the dangers posed by sexuality, the more it would have to be hidden, but then the more tantalising it would be. Alain's arrival was a breach in my defences, and they had to be shored up.

The next day I went to Cambridge with Caroline G and we spent a delightful three days being completely middle-aged, sitting in chapels listening to choirs, sipping from china cups in tearooms, applauding at the end of symphonies, sleeping in the awful college beds which would soon be my regular place of rest. I don't remember sharing the story of Alain with her – perhaps I was trying to unthink him out of existence. In any case, surely he'd be gone when I got home?

But this ploy had failed with Mark Sykes, and guess what…?

Caroline and I got off the bus from the station on our return from Cambridge and there, coming out of the Co-op with a carrier bag of groceries, was Alain. There was something of the busy housewife about him. When he saw me, a slightly bitter expression narrowed his eyes and tightened his mouth. He came across to us.

'Oh, you are return.' I think he was speaking English in deference to Caroline G. He pursed his lips. 'I am live 'ere still. I 'ave friend 'ere now. I meet in poob. But I 'ave no more money soon.' He shook the carrier bag towards us. 'Tomorrow, okay, you bring me breakfast. At the river, okay?'

He walked away towards the bottom of the market place, dignified in his suffering. Of course then I had to tell Caroline G who he was, but I gave her the edited version. We weren't the sort of friends who told each other absolutely everything. In spite of our kissing sessions (long over now, and which in any case had taken place in a sort of alternative universe and were never *ever* referred to in our normal world), she had a carefully polished veneer of innocence that kept her safe from undesirable knowledge; where I read the *NME* and my mum's *Cosmo*, she had her *Bunty*. She might have half a dozen boys dreaming of putting their hands down her bra, but she was not the sort of girl to let a man come all over her in the woods (unless she wasn't telling either). She seemed rather envious of my devoted Frenchman and fell silent on the walk home from town.

Seven o'clock the next morning, feeling just like Little Red Riding Hood, I slipped quietly out of the house. I actually had a basket! I had packed a thermos of Nescafé, some egg sandwiches and some fruit, including that day's precious single strawberry from the garden. I went down through the steep woods, past the place where Alain had come on me, to the river. Looking down, you could see the blue tent pitched by a bend, just beyond a bridge. Perhaps Alain, troll-like, had some special affinity with bridges.

Swinging my basket, I walked up to the tent. There was no sign of the wolf. Then I heard branches rustling and Alain emerged from the undergrowth holding a loo roll. Somehow I had imagined that air-force training would have eliminated the need for such things. Next he shaved with a battery-powered razor. We had hardly said anything to each other so far. I got the feeling that he was gathering his thoughts. I too was silently rehearsing what I was going to say to him to get him to go home. I was getting really spooked by his persistence.

The basket of breakfast was untouched on the ground. Patting his cheeks, Alain seemed to decide to make his move.

'*Alors*, Carrie, why won't you sleep with me?' In French now and with much more power at his disposal. 'Come on, *please*, now, in the tent…'

Oh no. Smiling my special smile of rejection, I shook my head. I felt nothing for this boy; I wasn't going to have to sleep with him merely out of guilt, was I? Surely not.

'*Allez*…' Wheedling, coaxing, Alain began to try to undo my shirt. I knew if I went into the tent, that would be as good as saying yes, so I stayed where I was, sitting on the damp grass, blocking him with my slumped shoulders. All this carry-on, all this stupid carry-on, just because of one night out at a disco.

There was truly the smell of punishment about it. I stared down at the ground.

'You're nothing but a cockteaser! I'm sick of it!' Alain picked up the paperback he'd been reading and hurled it into the bushes. 'Go on, just go, why don't you?' I got up and, picking up the basket, started to walk away over the boulders by the edge of the river. It was hard not to try to run, just to get away from the horrible accusing silence. I stumbled on until I got back to the road and the hill that led home. I felt really stupid with the basket. Somewhere along the line I must have done something wrong: this was surely a situation with the potential to be romantic, to be wonderful, but it was just alienating and embarrassing, as usual. If only I could have learnt the lesson right then, when I was only eighteen, that someone liking you doesn't mean you will like them, and that opening yourself up, even a little, to someone can bring a gushing torrent of unwanted attention, and spunk, onto you.

A few days later Mum came back from the shops with news. Alain's new 'friend', apparently, was the vicar's daughter! My mother had just met the vicar in town and he had told her that Sarah had seen Alain off the day before, as he got on the bus headed for the motorway so that he could hitchhike back down south.

The final word from Alain came in a letter, the handwriting so crabbed as to be barely legible, in which he expressed his profound bitterness that I had not reciprocated his love. At the time, I was so relieved that it was over, I didn't struggle to decode much more of the letter and now I find it almost impossible to decipher. There's one passage in an earlier letter that I have just managed to translate in which he says I have only one physical flaw: a fat bottom. 'You have no muscles. Go swimming, jog – that makes girls pretty. I adore everything else about you.' The seriousness with which he makes this comment, guaranteed to embarrass and annoy me, was of a piece with the possessive, somewhat high-handed tone of all the half dozen or so letters he wrote to me before I sent him packing. After so long, it's quite thrilling to see how many times he wrote 'Je t'aime', that iconic phrase. I can allow myself to think, now, 'Wow, a Frenchman fell in love with you.' But, really, if that was love, it was no better than candyfloss, whipped up out of nothing, its sweetness dissolving to lacerating needles.

Chapter 8

LOSING IT

I assume you're breaking lots of hearts. I remember thinking how noble and good I was to forgive you your indiscretion of leading me on ... I can remember you only faintly. I never really got to know you at all. You can't have been all frivolity.

From a letter to me, 14 February 1983 (age 20)

AT last, at last, at last, after what seemed like forever, I was at Cambridge University. I had been waiting for this for years; not just since I had passed the entrance exam, already nearly two years ago now, but since I had first decided that I wanted to be a student at Cambridge and not just a tourist, back when I used to visit the town during summer holidays with my great-aunt Peg, who lived in the Fens. Half a lifetime of waiting and now I was in.

The wrong bicycle with its tartan saddlebag and white rubber wheels was parked outside the college gates. I could have got a great old bike from the police auction like everybody else did, but I knew it would hurt my dad, so I didn't.

I had a 'set' of two rooms – a study with a shiny black-leather Chesterfield sofa and a bedroom with a bed that was even more badly sprung than my bed at home. My French plates were put away in the little pantry outside my rooms. I could hardly have guessed that, in a few weeks' time, after a very nice tea party, the moody Welsh girl who had the rooms above mine would help me with the washing up and then, apparently as some sort of experiment, stand in the kitchen holding my plates in a big stack and simply open her hands, so that most of them shattered on the floor.

My musty second-hand French books lined my shelves. I even had the book that Alain had thrown into the bushes on that terrible morning – I had gone down to the river after hearing that he had left, to reassure myself that he really had gone, and when I looked among the rosebay willowherb, the book was still there, the pages splayed open with damp. It was a collection of stories by the nineteenth-century Romantic writer Gerard de Nerval, including the beautiful *Sylvie*, about the author's obsessive love for a chimera from the past. When we came to study *Sylvie* as part of my course, I used that copy of the text. It was a cheap French paperback edition with the edges of the pages coloured yellow, quite different in feel from the annotated academic editions I usually used. That Frenchness, plus the fact that it had belonged to Alain, who had claimed to love me, gave it an extra layer of significance.

I had looked forward to starting at Cambridge for so long and so intensely that, as soon as I got there, I felt I belonged, or at least that I would be able to make myself a place. I was determined to. My strong desire to fit in and find a niche conflicted somewhat with my sense that in many ways the university was a rather class-ridden backwater of snobbery dressed up as tradition. My response was to find my way, cautiously at first, into the many-tentacled embrace of the University Left. At first, I was too politically naïve to understand that the Left in Cambridge (as everywhere else) was divided into many factions, often as distrustful of each other as they were of the despised Tories. All I had known of politics up till then was the street-cred leftiness of the *NME*, the right-on brotherhood of the Anti-Nazi League. I hadn't even voted in an election yet, but of course I hated Maggie – that went without saying.

I went to the Freshers' Week Fair, where all the university clubs and societies had stalls and tried to get you to sign up for membership. Most were horribly twee – Winnie the Pooh Soc, Rupert Brooke Soc, The Gilbert and Sullivan Society – but I liked the look of the boy who was on the Labour Students stall so I took the leaflet listing their events for the term. I decided I would attend, if only to see the boy again.

I don't think I realised at the time quite how pent-up my sexual feelings had been. I may even have gone a little mad. I have a bizarre memory, only partially repressed, of posing one day with a bicycle saddle I had in my room. The saddle was an 'art object', a Picasso-style bull's head that I kept on my mantelpiece. I was on my own and some strange mood came over me: I photographed myself naked with the saddle suggestively positioned between my open legs. I *might* have done the same with an iron… This was long before digital cameras, and I didn't have a Polaroid, so I suppose I must have been insane enough to send the film for developing. I have absolutely no memory of ever seeing the printed photos, thank God. Perhaps the photo company had a policy of not handling rude pictures and I never got them back; perhaps I have simply blanked the memory of them. Of course, these days they would probably win the Turner Prize.

The madness went on, now that total freedom had rushed in on me. I was gripped by a terrible curiosity to see penises. Not *real* ones, lordy no! But pictures. I really wanted to look at pictures of … cocks (probably not the word I would have used then; in truth I did not have a word for them – they were unnameable). Perhaps it was a throwback to my old *Mayfair* days

– not that there was the remotest chance of seeing a penis in the pages of *Mayfair*. But the idea that looking at visual pornography would be satisfying in itself, not just a poor substitute for the real thing, must have still been quite active within me.

Playgirl, that was the answer. I had never seen a copy of *Playgirl*, but I knew all about it (or I imagined I did): page after page of huge, fascinating dicks. The more I thought about it, the more I wanted to see it. I told myself again and again there was no law against buying a dirty magazine, but I still felt too shy to go into a newsagent's and buy a copy. But how I wanted to see it! Round and round the argument went in my head until, one Saturday morning, my desire to see male flesh got the better of my inhibitions. I unpadlocked the bicycle from outside the college gates and, sitting bolt upright, pedalled off to fetch my prize.

I had decided that the most anonymous place to buy *Playgirl* would be the railway station. Cambridge station is a long way from the centre of town and it took a while to cycle through the Saturday traffic up Hills Road – of course, being Cambridge there were no actual hills. I reached the station and parked the bike. I prayed I wouldn't see anyone I knew going home for the weekend or meeting a friend off a train. As I walked into WH Smith, I suddenly awoke from the fugue state that had got me this far. *What on earth was I doing?* But, no, even in a more rational state of mind, I thought I might as well buy *Playgirl* now that I was here. Was it so bad? I went over to the magazine racks and looked along the line of women's mags: *She, Cosmo, Woman's Own, Good Housekeeping…* No sign of *Playgirl*. I scanned the shelves, from bottom to … top. Oh god! There it was, on the top shelf with *Mayfair* and *Playboy* and *Razzle*. I *couldn't* reach up and get it, I just *couldn't*. It was that action of reaching up; everyone would see me, I would be branded a pervert! Look, there was some dirty bastard, right now, reaching up for *Mayfair*, glancing guiltily around as he did so, holding it face down once he'd got it. That would be me! But that was why I'd come all this way, to be a dirty girl in relative anonymity. *Go on!*

No, it was no good. I went and got a wire basket and wandered round the shop. It was only small and there wasn't much to buy. I chose a couple of birthday cards and then ... inspiration! A sheet of wrapping paper. I laid the paper, folded in four, on the bottom of the basket, then, in a movement which I hoped was so swift and slick as to go unnoticed, I palmed a copy of *Playgirl* and concealed it under the wrapping paper. Brilliant. Then all I had to do was stand in the queue at the till, stare steadfastly into the middle distance, hand over some money, and I was out, with a WH Smith carrier bag to hide my shame. It wasn't quite euphoria that swept me back to college, but there was a definite tingle of achievement to quicken my pedalling – and of course the anticipation of discovering what lay within the naughty magazine's pages.

Once back in my study, the door locked, I put the *Playgirl* on my desk and began to turn the pages. It was a horrible letdown. My *courage*, my *quest* – and the reward was this pitiful collection of half-hidden, flaccid nubs. Shirtless boys with multicoloured bow-ties and lacquered hair smiled through lip-glossed lips – they reminded me very much of Caroline G. Buttocks, yes, muscled chests, yes, but so what? I was in search of sexological enlightenment: *where were the big dicks?* Small, small, small, not to say puny. The rule of thumb seemed to be that the more you could see, the smaller the actual picture had to be. The only pictures which had the faintest whiff of transgression about them were from a report about a nude rodeo in America. Grizzled middle-aged men in cutaway leather chaps rode around on horses under an uncharacteristically overcast Texas sky. Either cold or fear had shrivelled their cocks to grey whelks, but there was something titillatingly freaky about their desire to sit astride these big, unruly animals with no pants on. The rest of the magazine was just a brightly coloured tease. I cut out all the little penises – the madness was definitely still upon me – castrating their cowboy owners so that I was left with a few inch-square scraps of paper, which I put into a little clear-plastic wallet. Then I threw away the stupid magazine and tried to think about something else.

With hindsight, I reached this peak of sexual curiosity about twenty years too soon. Nowadays you can see anything that takes your fancy, from any angle, in any combination, for free and without relinquishing your anonymity, on the Internet. Back then, I could come up with nothing better than this limp comic. Oh, I know there were (still are) laws about what you could show, and WH Smith, that great guardian of our morality, was selling it, so how explicit could it have been? But it was pathetic!

I began to feel differently about boys – real, physical, fleshly boys – now that I had left home. My horrible hang-up about letting my parents know I was interested in sex held no sway in Cambridge. I could do as I liked. That the college authorities officially frowned on sexual activity more than my parents ever had meant little. I didn't have a hang-up about *them*, and anyway it was universally understood that in practice the colleges turned a benevolently blind eye to student sex. I was definitely on for it now. Well, at least more on for it than I had ever been before.

I wasn't the only first-year in a state of febrile sexual tension. The student accommodation was in a many-angled court, and my ground-floor study faced another across a ninety-degree corner. The window in front of my desk looked across to the desk in the room opposite. The occupant of this room was an intense, very overweight boy called Philip who, because of our proximity, had soon become a friend, along with the odd plate-smashing Welsh girl upstairs. I had already had to comfort him after the murder of John Lennon, when I had found him keening on the stairs outside. (I felt guilty because I didn't feel emotional about his death; I'd never been into the Beatles.) And one afternoon he had come and asked if he could play some records on my music centre, which I was still very proud of even though it was as big as a raft. I had said yes, not realising in time that this would entail him lying upside-down on my bed with his bare fat-boy feet on my pillow while he listened through my headphones and sang along discordantly. I had also fed him Brie one evening, half aware that this intimate little supper was having a seductive effect on him that I didn't intend. Or did the coquette know exactly what she was doing, yet not want to have to deal with any consequences?

It was late one night when Philip knocked on my door. He, of course, knew that I was still up because he could see the light in my window.

'Can I read you something I've written?'

I let him in. I had fallen into the irregular and unpredictable rhythms of student life with enthusiasm. He sat down on the sofa and began to read me a short story about a student whose room looks into the room of a girl student: he watches her messing about with her boyfriend, flirting with him, kissing him, then he stands at his window and shoots them both.

There were no more Brie suppers for Philip after that.

For the first event of the Labour Students' programme, Ray

Buckton, the leader of ASLEF, the train drivers' union, was coming to talk to the earnest Labour-supporting swots. Never had anything appealed to me less. But I went because, in the few seconds that I had stood in front of him and picked up a badge and a leaflet, I had sensed an unspoken exchange between me and the boy on the Labour Students stall.

The meeting was being held in a fabulously ornate Pugin-style room in one of the colleges. There at a table looking faintly grimy and smut-stained, as though he had just driven himself to Cambridge at the wheel of a great steam engine, was the chief train driver; and there, next to him, was the boy! He was obviously important! I sat down in an empty row of chairs – most of the rows were empty, Mr Buckton apparently not being a big draw among Cambridge's bright young things – and the boy saw me and smiled. He was wearing a checked shirt with the sleeves rolled up in what I thought was a rather too obviously 'proletarian' way, but maybe when you were a Cambridge student you had to underline your socialist leanings a little more deliberately than other students.

When the turnout had just scraped above embarrassing (I would discover in the weeks to come that virtually everyone else present that day was already a stalwart of the student Left – I represented high-value new blood) the boy introduced Mr Buckton. I liked his jolly London-accented voice with its hint of just-suppressed mockery. Then Mr Buckton spoke, at length, about … well, who knows what about? Trains, perhaps. It was impossible for me to take it in, not because I was lost in fantasies about the boy – no, I was really trying to concentrate – but it was just so *phenomenally* boring that my brain shut down. I came to and realised that the boy was asking the audience if they had any questions. *No one* had any questions. The boy's eyes swept the room, he smiled slightly less engagingly than before, the fun tempered by a hint of exasperation. He looked at me. I so wanted to help him. I had no idea what I could ask. I put my hand up and he nodded happily at me.

'Yes? You've got a question?'

No, but here goes. 'Erm, would you say... that... we'll ever see... er ... privatisation of the railways?' *Yes! I'd done it!* Cupid's arrow had landed in a hitherto dormant lobe of my brain and electric-shocked a question about *railways* out of my mouth. The boy beamed at me. Mr Buckton was giving his answer but I didn't hear it.

The meeting ended swiftly after that, and as chairs were being dragged back and Ray Buckton was putting his donkey jacket back on, the boy came over to me, grinning.

'Thanks for that – saved my skin.'

I smiled back. 'Oh, you know, it was just a question.'

He seemed to remember his important role in the Labour Students. 'I'm Ben, by the way, Ben Tilman, and you're...?'

'Carrie Jones.'

'Well, Carrie, I hope we'll be seeing you at more Labour Students events. You should come to our lunches.' A thought seemed to occur to him. 'D'you want to come to a party? We're having a party on my staircase, tomorrow night. M staircase, St Saviour's.'

'Okay. Yeah, okay, see you there then.' I was trying to be cool but as I cycled back to college I was grinning so madly I had to wipe dead midges off my teeth.

By the next evening when I had to go to the party on my own, the weather had changed and it had suddenly become desperately cold, the wind striking in across the Fens from the east. But a party was a party. It was the height of New Romanticism;

Adam Ant swung into the charts every week through a plate-glass window or on the end of a pirate rope with a cutlass between his teeth. The fashion was all cheap frills. I had a white shirt with a huge, frothing ruffle all down the front, a fuchsia-pink ra-ra skirt, and a pair of royal-blue high-heeled ankle boots with beaded fringes. My eyelids burnished with silver eyeshadow and my lashes laden with bright-blue mascara, I pulled on the boots, threw on a coat and set off to the party. It was about nine o'clock – not late enough to make a really dramatic entrance, but I just couldn't wait any longer.

I had been going to ride my bike, as usual, but ice was already sparkling on the roads and I decided to walk. It wasn't very far to St Saviour's College.

I will never forget what it felt like to be walking along in those beaded boots to that party on M Staircase. I was nervous and yet I was an all-conquering Amazon. The idiotic boots had no grip in the soles and I kept slipping, nearly falling over, and yet they also made me feel as lithe as a jaguar. I knew, I just knew, that I was going to connect with Ben Tilman at the party and that knowledge made me powerful, even if it was scary to be going alone to a party where I didn't know anyone.

When Sylvia Plath first met Ted Hughes it was at a party in Cambridge. She saw him for the first time, went up to him, and bit him on the cheek. She drew blood. I wish I could lay claim to such glamorous intensity, but I had to accept a less feral coming together. By the time I had tottered round to St Saviour's, slunk past the porters' lodge (St Saviour's had been founded in a rather disapproving Methodist tradition and the porters seemed to have been specially bred to uphold the stern values of the founders), and found the right staircase, which was easy because such loud music was rocking out of it, I was feeling acutely self-conscious. Couples were kissing; little groups were smoking and laughing. I kept walking, further and further down the corridor, looking into the open doors of all the rooms, until I saw Ben. There was no *coup de foudre*, he was too straightforward for that, but he was definitely pleased to see me. He got me a glass of wine and then I just stood next to him for the rest of the evening, like a wife of many years' standing. He introduced me to his friends. I smiled a lot. We didn't talk much on our own, but I didn't mind. I laughed at everybody's jokes – it was all jokes – and gradually it seemed to be accepted that I was 'with' Ben. A girl nudged me and said, 'You staying the night, then?'

It was late and people were leaving. The music had had to be turned down. Ben had a slightly fatherly manner, I'd noticed. He possibly had a tendency to be a tiny bit patronising, but he was nice, really nice. I liked him a lot. And he was a third-year. And in charge of the Labour Students. If he wanted me, I would have him.

He came over to me after a turn around the room to collect empties. 'Better get yourself home, then.'

Oh Sylvia, Sylvia, I needed your fox-sharp little teeth, I needed your madness. I looked down at the fringed boots. 'Yes, I suppose I had.'

Ben nodded. 'Okay. I'll see you soon. What about tomorrow night? I'll cook something and we could go to the pictures. There's a Kurosawa film on.'

I had absolutely no idea who or what Kurosawa was, but I said yes. Then I walked back down through the drunken people on the stairs, through the little Alice-in-Wonderland door cut in the heavy wooden gates of the college, which were now shut, and back along the frosted road to my own college. The boots were really hurting now, but there was a sashaying swing to my step: I had got my man. Nearly.

Frozen fillets of fish shaped like oven gloves, frozen chips and frozen peas. This was the arctic feast Ben cooked for me the next evening. His best friend Hal, who lived in the next-door room, came and talked to us while we were in the kitchen, but then we went into Ben's room and ate our food on our knees. He told me about the campaigns he was planning. All this politicking impressed me. I found it attractive too. That Socialist Students badge he wore was shorthand for a whole load of traits; it took away a lot of the risk involved in selecting a boyfriend. He was a member of a tribe. He had the haircut, he wore the shirt, he liked the music – and that made him seem safe but also good.

We cycled to the cinema and I found out that Akira Kurosawa made epic Samurai films. My instinct was to turn up my nose, but I gathered from Ben's respectful enthusiasm that there was more to it than mere swashbuckling. Kurosawa did *literary* swashbuckling, *allegorical* swashbuckling, so I had better pay attention and try to appreciate the subtleties that underlay the flailing swords and leaping warriors. It was his new film, *Kagemusha*, but I failed to become even the tiniest bit absorbed in what was happening on the screen. At first there was the exquisite anticipation that Ben might take my hand, perhaps even kiss me, to distract me from the onscreen action; but then my stomach began to take over as the only focus of my attention. Perhaps Ben hadn't thawed out the frozen mitts of cod properly, perhaps they had been crammed in the freezer compartment of his shared student fridge for too many months, perhaps it was just nerves, but I had the most terrible stomach ache I had ever experienced. It was trying to rip the flesh away from my ribs; it would liquidate my guts and then move inexorably on to my other organs. I rocked back and forth on my red plush seat as discreetly as I could to try to soothe myself but it was no good. Ben hadn't noticed that anything was wrong with me. He was sombrely absorbed in the film. At least the shrieks and gasps of the soundtrack permitted me a few moans of my own, but the thundering decibels were too much. I felt as though the noise was crushing me. I patted Ben on the arm – he had them very sensibly folded. I was beginning to discover that he wasn't the most romantic of boyfriends.

'I'm going to have to go home,' I said into his ear, enjoying the brush of my lips against his skin in spite of everything. I pointed exaggeratedly at my stomach, 'Terrible stomach ache. Sorry.'

Ben made a sad face and shrugged. It occurred to me that if he was really crazy about me he might have left the cinema to attend to me as I slipped into the final stages of acute appendicitis, but no, he was far too sensible for that.

'Okay. I'll see you soon,' and his eyes refocused on the teeming screen.

I cycled back to my college rooms, bent low over the handlebars of my bike to minimise the strain on my drum-tight stomach. Bob Dylan tangled with Janis Ian and Wagner as I curled up in the bottom of my boat-bed and listened to other people's Sunday evenings coming through the walls and ceiling.

It didn't seem so at the time, but really it was lucky for me that Ben was such a decent, straightforward person. He was not just fatherly, he was verging on the avuncular, so patient and undemanding was his courtship of me. Not many third-year students, with a couple of years of sexual freedom under their belts, would have waited for so long while I prepared myself mentally and physically for the loss, or rather, the careful putting aside of my virginity.

Carrie Jones

The fact that I was still a virgin was no secret. It had already come to light in the course of one of those over-frank conversations which take place when people who know nothing about each other find themselves in a room late one night and lose all their inhibitions. In my case, I had spent virtually every night of my first few weeks as a student crammed in other people's rooms, drinking undrinkable coffee and spraying out intimate details about myself to anyone who could hear me above the noise of other people being similarly indiscreet. Was there anyone in the first year who did not know that Sonia Bragg had lost her virginity in the toilets at Lord's, or that Matilda Grey had a third nipple? Garth O'Donohue's experiments with mushrooms were common knowledge, as was Paul Dryden's masturbatory obsession with Toyah. I, in my turn, had spun out the story of French Alain to maximum effect and had gladly admitted to still being a virgin since it prolonged the gorgeous sensation of being the centre of laughing, admiring attention for a little longer. I wasn't too pleased when Malcolm Sanderson, who had already used *his* moment centre-stage to declare that he had recently decided he was gay, came over a little later and offered to sleep with me, 'just so that I would know what it was like'. I had gambled and decided to wait for a better offer. Now it looked as though my steadfastness was going to pay off.

It was well into my second term at Cambridge (following the Christmas break during which Ben had written me a cheerful letter about his North London home life and had managed not even to hint at our romantic attachment) when I began to detect a mild and unthreatening impatience on his part. Perhaps I might like to stay over one night after one of our pleasant and friendly evenings together rather than slipping out through the little door in the college gates and cycling home in the icy night air? Oh we kissed, lots and lots, and I liked to sit on his lap in the Ercol armchair in his room and stroke his lovely soft black hair, but things had never reached the sort of pitch to allow us to forget ourselves and tumble into bed. Perhaps it seems as though I was trying have it both ways; that it was no good being alarmed by hot-blooded men when they came on strong and then resenting Ben's good and gentle consideration. But rather than comparing, say, querulous Alain with patient Ben, the contrast I felt more keenly was between the dreamy yet intense romanticism of how I had *imagined* sex would be and the politeness of my *actual* sexual progress. It was all so terribly sensible.

It was sensible, too,to get myself a prescription for the Pill, before I made the leap into Ben's bed (although 'leap' suggested a move with far more energy and abandon than either of us seemed to possess). I made an appointment with the doctor in town to whose list my name had been added on my arrival at the University.

On a cold February morning in 1981 I cycled to the surgery and waited for my name to be called. It was quite a shock to be sitting in the waiting room with townspeople — fidgety children, their cheeks flushed with fever, emphysemic old men and swollen-ankled old ladies — and I was suddenly conscious of the degree to which we students lived a separate existence from the population of Cambridge. It often seemed that, apart from the vigorous young students, the only other citizens were the college porters (bluff, stony-faced men) and the 'bedders', pursed-lipped women who came into our rooms every day to empty our waste-paper bins and make clear their disapproval of our self-indulgent, indolent lives; even the dons were mostly invisible, just a flap of gown disappearing into a staircase. Increasingly self-conscious, I read my Italian novel until my turn came.

Carrie Jones

Stiffly the doctor called me into his room. Sitting down, I took care to keep my knees together. I did not want to give any hint of wantonness. My request for the contraceptive pill was to seem serious, carefully thought out and wholly unrelated to any desire on my part for fun, pleasure or, god forbid, sexual satisfaction. I was concise to the point of brusqueness. I was scared this stale-looking man would question me about the state of my 'relationship', my reasons for wanting contraception, my moral fibre. I wouldn't have had any convincing answers. I wasn't even quite sure that, as a student, I was *allowed* to have sex. But the fact was that I was an adult and (as usual) I was being 'sensible' in seeking contraception, and this was years before HIV and Aids, so there was no pressure to protect yourself from infection with condoms. In those days there was very little concern about the side-effects of the Pill either. After the doctor had taken my blood pressure and weighed me, I got the prescription and was soon in possession of a six-month supply of chemical prophylactic.

I felt light-headed – with relief that my enforced contact with authority was done with – but as the day went on the light-headed feeling was prolonged by the bubbling up of euphoria: I had done it, I had climbed the fence and jumped down to the other side. I was in among the *doers* and no longer just staring in from among the herds of dreamers and fantasisers. I didn't know what sex was actually like, or for, but I now had the passport to that strange country.

My effervescent mood had a strange effect: it emanated from me and communicated itself to some of the most eccentric people in my college, drawing them to my rooms for a surreal evening of drinking and hysteria. Two or three students, who were barely ever seen about the college, and whose names I hardly knew, were somehow caught up in the swirls of energy released by my newly adult status. These were boys who I would normally not even have looked at, boys with hair like Cleopatra, boys whose only release from the agony of not fitting in to any of the college tribes was to spend hours on the ancient pinball machine in the darkest corner of the college bar. Like the Pied Piper of Hamelin, I drew them out of their rat-holes and led them back to my rooms, where I dished out college port, a kind of lethally alcoholic Ribena. I think I even tried a drag on a cigarette, so far along the pirate plank of adult vice had I ventured (of course I hated it). Nothing overtly sexual happened during this odd evening — I was celebrating my transgression and those boys, given their pariah status, were lucky to have been admitted to the baby Bacchanalia; it never happened again.

I didn't see Ben that night, nor for the next few days. The next time I visited his room in St Saviour's I whispered shyly in his ear that I was now on the Pill. It would have been much better to have waited before telling him this most unromantic of news until the magic hormones had started to do their work and I was 'ready to go'. As it was, we now had to wait a couple more weeks until I was officially baby-proof. This had the effect of starting a kind of creepy countdown to the night when my notional hymen could finally be breached (Tampax had already done for the real thing, I imagined). Thus any chance of spontaneity or impulsive gesture was bypassed: this was planned non-parenthood.

Still, I think Ben was pleased. He had waited patiently for me to decide it was 'time' — partly, of course, because he was a 'new man' and very aware of the political correctness of it being my choice (he wasn't one of the leading lights of the University Left for nothing). But I think he really loved the idea of being the man who initiated me into fully fledged sex, of being the *first*. Also, Ben was very particular about hygiene. He was always cleaning up after the other students in the kitchen or doing huge washes in the launderette, and no doubt my shiny virgin state appealed to that aspect of him too.

So, the day came. I was working hard on an essay, but at about ten I cycled round to St Saviour's. There was something grim about my exaggerated self-awareness, an almost filmic, watching-myself-from-above sense of doom as I walked quietly down the corridor to the end room, the room from which I would emerge 'a woman'.

God. How do you *do* this stuff without the child that you are screeching with laughter and pointing (*'Ugh, what's that?'*) – or else just curling up in fear? How do you act grown-up when it really matters? You gather yourself together at the door, stare at the grain of the wood for a few seconds, mentally smooth down your skirt, then knock softly. You're a character in your own drama; it's not Thomas Hardy, nor is it Jane Austen... It's maybe more like Mike Leigh. You smile when Ben turns round at his desk. You go over and put your arms around him from behind and kiss his soft hair. Then you curl up in the armchair while he finishes what he's doing. You're not thinking too far ahead, you don't want to start worrying about whether it's going to hurt. *Is it going to hurt?* Try to look dignified, if you can't manage sultry.

Ben closes his books and goes to make mugs of tea. I am glad to have the hot tea to hold and the rim of the mug to look over. I am really quite worried about this. The question of whether I'm going to enjoy it has been pushed way down the queue by other less polite questions: am I going to take all my clothes off? Should I have brought a nightie? (I've brought my toothbrush.) What if I want to go to the loo in the night? How are we going to fit into the neat single bed? What if the 'bedder' catches us in the morning? Is it really worth it?

Deciding to sleep with Ben wasn't about being in love with him. I did like him, very much, and it felt good to be his girlfriend — and his friend — but there wasn't that obsessive fetishising lust which, for me, only seems to get a hold when I can't have the object of my desire straight away. No, this was about joining a club, doing something that everybody else was doing so that I could feel allied with them, not different. I didn't feel any desire. I applied the same self-discipline which I would switch on for my first driving lesson a few years later, a deliberate strategy of concentration and heightened self-control designed to combat nervousness and avoid accidents.

We make a pretence of chatting as if this is just a normal late-night visit. Then Ben stands up and takes my hand. We go into his bedroom, where I have hardly ever been before now. It's neat and simple. The bed is very severely made and I imagine the woman who made it, her muscles overdeveloped from years of trying to turn tucked-in sheets into a viable form of contraception. Would this same woman discover me tomorrow, the ruiner of her hospital corners, Goldilocks still in Baby Bear's bed? The lamp is on in the other room, but Ben thoughtfully leaves the light off in the bedroom. He's helping me out of my clothes. In the state of mind I'm in, this isn't sexy, it's more like receiving the attention of a kindly nurse after being slightly hurt in a bus crash. Oh yes, kissing, I'm supposed to do kissing as well. It takes a bit of effort for Ben to undo the invisible bolts that are holding the sheets together, but then the inner layers of the bed are folded out to receive their filling. And I must receive mine too. Through the taut threads of my 'preparedness' there does now weave a more sensuous, undulating weft of pleasure, wisps of feeling which hint at something that might be more intensely enjoyed in the future. It's good to be lying down with Ben, to feel more skin against skin than I have ever felt before, and to feel that I am with someone who cares about me. But here we go. Without much preliminary, Ben is pushing himself into me, and I have to draw up my legs. And … yes, it *does* hurt, *ah*, really quite a lot, an oxymoronic sharp-dull pain that is offset by the movement and the presence of new flesh in my flesh. It's weird, all my fantasies about what it will be like when I finally have sex with someone have been about the *feeling*, how I am going to enjoy the feeling of a penis, maybe I'm even going to feel as though I'm getting that penis for myself, borrowing some of its power. But now that it's actually happening, I can't *really* feel it – I know it's there, but the feeling is all at the point of entry; it's as if there's nothing beyond the gateway into my body but a black hole.

Before I begin to be conscious of wishing that it would stop, it stops. Ben groans and relaxes. He kisses me and asks me if I'm alright. I am alright. Before long he delicately separates himself from me and settles around me in the narrow bed to sleep. I look into the near darkness and wish we had turned off the lamp in the other room. The gleam of its light seems to be intensifying, penetrating beneath my eyelids when I close them. I turn my face into the pillow and try to sleep. I can feel the impression in my flesh of the thrusts Ben made and now, with a tiny spasm like a capsule bursting, I feel the glug of Ben's sperm leaving my body. I've made my first wet patch.

Chapter 9

COLD FISH

Sexual desire is sinful because it asserts the individual's own sexuality and separates him from the mother, makes him other ... sexual desire is the essence of personality.

Notes on Proust in a notebook from 1983 (age 20)

BEING sexually active was a powerful tool. The knowledge that I could now add my willingness to sleep with someone to my arsenal of boyfriend-bagging ammunition made me feel very different. It became harder and harder to keep going with trusty Ben when there were so many other appealing boys around. Then, while Ben was having to immerse himself in work for his finals, I did something guaranteed to drive us apart.

Dinner parties were all the rage amongst the students, but the food that was served and the manner in which it had to be eaten always seemed to undermine the elegant ambitions of the host or hostess. The food I ate at student dinner parties has never been surpassed for nastiness: heaps of brown rice flavoured with raw ginger; steak tartare with a raw egg congealing in the centre of each plate (although I think this dish was actually intended as some sort of Dadaist happening); a tin of Campbell's mushroom soup bulked out with a tin of sweetcorn and a tin of tuna; lasagne which cracked audibly as the serving spoon broke through the uncooked pasta layers (I confess – this last was my own disaster).

Ben threw a dinner party that went delightfully well. We had all managed to balance our plates of ratatouille on the arms of our Ercol armchairs (brought in specially from each room along the corridor and lined up along the walls). We had even managed to eat most of it. Then Ben handed each of us a white plastic cup containing a dollop of cottage cheese sitting in a pool of espresso coffee. It looked disgusting, it smelt disgusting, and it tasted disgusting. But Ben had made it and Ben was my boyfriend so I loyally gulped it down. Everyone else seemed to love it.

Later that night, after Ben had washed up, dried the dishes, wiped down the surfaces and hung out the damp tea-towel, we went to bed and after a brief, slightly drunken coupling, fell asleep. Minutes later, I woke up and knew at once that the coffee-stained granules of cheese were about to make a second appearance. There was no time to reach the bathroom, I only just made it to Ben's bedroom hand basin. The misery of throwing up was quickly blotted out by my terror when I realised I had blocked the sink. As I stared at the gross evidence of my malfunctioning innards, I heard Ben's breathing falter, then fall into regularity again. Still asleep, thank God. I tried turning on the tap but the addition of water simply swelled the volume of the swirling, reeking horror. Gurning with distaste, I poked at the plughole with the handle end of my toothbrush. By dribbling a tiny flow of water into the sink and working at the heaps of undigested cheese settling over the plug, I eventually managed to make them disappear. There still seemed to be a rank smell of coffee, or was that just the sour burn in my throat? Reluctantly I brushed my teeth with the defiled toothbrush and crept back into bed. Ben's head had lolled over to my side, so I lay with my face hanging over the edge of the mattress. It was all I deserved – I felt that I should be punished for fouling his clean, orderly nest. I slept like a frozen sentry laid on his side to thaw out. In spite of the narrow single bed, barely any part of me touched Ben – even though he had slept through the whole thing, I knew that's how he'd want it to be.

In the morning, Ben woke up and went smartly to the basin to brush his teeth. I pretended to doze but I was lying rigidly to attention: would there be a problem with the sink?

"Ugh! The sink's blocked! *Eughh!*"

It was just as bad as I'd imagined. Ben was horrified when a brackish liquid crept back up from the plughole as he busily polished his teeth. I had to confess my crime, of course, and he was unable to mask his distaste.

I don't remember a formal parting ceremony. I simply transferred my allegiance from Ben to Sean, a University Left comrade-in-arms. In fact, I remember the actual moment of transfer. Late one night Ben had been round at my rooms for a half-hearted coffee on the black-leather Chesterfield sofa and, moments after he left, there was a tap at the sash-window. I opened it and, thrillingly, in climbed Sean, saving himself the trouble of going round to the back of the building to get in through the underground bike store (the gates were closed at midnight). The sight of his thighs rolling over the windowsill landed Sean the role of Milk Tray Man in my imagination, even though, in reality, he was a thin-lipped Marxist who would soon be giving me the cold shoulder for not being up to scratch on Rosa Luxemburg.

The big mistake I made was to choose my boyfriends from the limited and rather icy pool of the University Left. Some students threw themselves into forming a band, or amateur dramatics; others became obsessed with rowing; other still-maturing minds became lost in the all-too-real-seeming underworld of Dungeons and Dragons. But the boys I knew were seriously caught up in a joyless left-wing fervour that found them nightly bent over the Letraset, producing leaflets destined to lie unread in ten thousand pigeonholes. Almost every lunchtime they would get together in a stale room in King's or Catz, dropping their comradely 50p into a suitably proletarian beer mug stolen from a pub and munching on doorsteps of bread and cheese while they discussed the latest campaign.

Along with a few other girls who were willing to put up with the austere and humourless atmosphere, I was a Marianne to these *sans-culottes*, happy to man the barricades if it meant there was a bit of shouting and a cheery celebration in the pub afterwards. In my scrapbook there are many yellowing newspaper photos of sit-ins and demos in which I can identify myself. I'm not usually centre-stage, and there is often an angrily jabbing hand in front of my face, or a banner, so it's a question of recognising the bulge of my thighs in their skin-tight drainpipe jeans, or the cut of my anorak hood, pulled up to keep out the snow or rain. In one of the few photos where my face is clearly visible, I look just like my granny, in a fluffy tea-cosy hat and matching scarf. Only men who were fatally entangled in the web of anti-sexism and gender politics could desire such frumpiness.

Of course, 'desire' as such had to be suppressed – sexual relations among the Cambridge comrades were about mutual respect, total equality, non-exploitation, although in practice it was still the boys who stood up and did most of the pontificating. They all took it so terribly seriously; with hindsight, I wish I had tried to join the Footlights or hung out with the arty set, but I had dug myself deep into the lefty trenches. I *did* support the causes. I really did want to Stop The Cuts and wreck the student-organised beauty contest – "They're only out there cos they're not pretty" runs the headline on the press-cutting of that demo – but my political convictions were built on the thinnest veneer of informed awareness, shored up by a gut-sense of right-on rightness, and powered by a fatal attraction to these skinny, high-voiced would-be Che Guevaras.

If you were going out with a lefty, there was a strict code of conduct. Rule One was that absolutely no affection should be shown between boyfriend and girlfriend during any official lefty business. A discreet loitering after meetings might be permitted, provided there was no physical contact, just a quick exchange to fix up whose room you would sleep at that night, yours or his. Only once did I break this protocol, when I foolishly submitted to the attentions of a brilliantly intelligent but uncharismatic law student and held his hand during a College Left bread-and-cheese lunch. I should have known he would bend the rules – he wasn't a *true* lefty but a very committed Liberal. All I could think about was the appalling state of his polyester sweater, which he was wearing straight from the tumble dryer. I managed to detach myself from his earnest fingers before there was any question of us sleeping together; only straight-down-the-line socialists earned my sexual allegiance. Besides, they were much better dressed. Oh, those raffish hats brought back from summers picking fair-trade coffee with the Sandinistas, those army surplus fatigues, those T-shirts handpainted with 'Support the Miners'.

So, yes, there was sex, lots of it, but it was strangely joyless. Perhaps the boys I went out with from the University Left had been rendered too self-conscious, too hung-up about whether they were 'sexist pigs', to allow themselves to show any pleasure. Perhaps it was also because sex was rather perfunctory, a late-night exercise to be carried out after all the rest of the day's business had been completed. In 'normal' student life there's a lot more hanging around together, eating, watching telly, going to the pub… It melds you together in a more natural way. As a student activist, there didn't seem to be time just to hang out. I spent every spare moment delivering leaflets to the entire student population. I prided myself on knowing the location of every single set of pigeonholes throughout the whole university, even the ones in the weird theological colleges and the colleges for mature students (although they didn't really count as students in our eyes, we were happy to harvest their votes in elections). I knew all the back ways between the colleges and accommodation blocks, the paths over streams and mill ponds, the cobbled cut-throughs. I was a premier-league leafletter. What did I care that most of the leaflets would be thrown away as soon as they were received?

So much dedication to the cause didn't leave much time for lingering love scenes. It was more a case of finishing my work at around 11pm or midnight and cycling round to my boyfriend's room like a lodger who is discouraged from hanging around on the premises except to sleep. Sean's room was in the basement of a huge, rundown house. He was lucky to have his own 'bathroom', but this dank, unheated storeroom with its filthy lavatory and industrial-sized sink was so depressing that it soon began to erode my enthusiasm for Sean himself. This was the first of many times still to come when some aspect of a boyfriend's lifestyle, not inherently a fault in the man himself, undermined the chances of my loving him for ever, or even at all. I must just be a sensitive soul with standards – or else a sad, shallow anal-retentive. Worse still, Sean couldn't sleep unless he had the World Service on all night – no doubt he was anxious not to miss news of a possible coup in El Salvador or Burkina Faso, or anywhere else he might be needed to take up arms. I still can't hear 'Lillibulero' without tensing up.

Who knows why some relationships last so much longer than others when all (mine, anyway) are doomed to fail? The seeds of failure sprout pretty early on – I think you are usually aware of the reasons why you will eventually dislike someone almost immediately, but it's perfectly possible to ignore the signs if your need for a lover is great. Let's face it, it usually is. You may have said to yourself, 'Well, I'm not too keen on his pet rat,' or, 'Hmm, I could do without the T-shaped goatee,' but then thought you would give it a whirl regardless. Never works, does it? Sooner or later, inexorably, the rodent will come to seem like Satan's own familiar, the facial fringing will really rub you up the wrong way. I once met someone and had immediate misgivings about him. Very unusually for me, when he asked me out I said no thanks. Whereupon he sent me a note, pleading his cause, in which he actually referred to himself as a 'Renaissance Man'! Worse still, I allowed myself to be persuaded and ended up living with this modern day da Vinci. But it all came to nothing, and the traits I had recoiled from at the outset were the very same things I wanted to escape when I dumped him, except that now I had a more intimate and detailed knowledge of them. Wouldn't it have been better not to have bothered?

Somewhere, carefully hidden, I've got a small notebook where, on one page, I have written down the names of all the men I've ever slept with, in the order in which I slept with them. There's a little coded dot beside each name for 'major relationship', 'someone I really liked but which didn't last long' or 'one-night stand'. When I married, it seemed important to put that book out of reach, although I never felt I should destroy it. In any case, when I slipped on the magic golden band I seemed to become invisible, and it seemed unlikely I would be making any new additions to the list. There were just a couple of dozen names or thereabouts on the list – they could have split into teams and played football against each other – but, with the notebook now lost, I find I'm no longer sure of the precise order in which they followed each other. The length and complexity of my involvements varied wildly, before slowing into a sequence of stately quasi-marriages and, finally, marriage. During my time at university, though, the merry-go-round twirled giddily, and some boys were flung off after one ride whilst some managed to cling on for a few turns.

I soon perfected the head-up, eyes-unfocused walk of phoney self-confidence that was necessary to get oneself out of a boyfriend's room and out of his house or college early in the morning. I would ignore the students standing around in the kitchen making toast. I chose not to see the porter bringing the post to the pigeonholes and shaking his head at the unauthorised female guest. Once on my bike and pedalling away to my first lecture, I was cut away from whatever clammy coupling had happened in the preceding hours. If you'd asked me, I would have said that sex was good because it was intimate, but, in truth, sometimes it made you feel further away from the other person than ever. There was so little engagement, in either direction, no talking about what felt good, no exploration. Sex was so much less than I wish it to be now, now that I no longer have the luxury of freedom and youth. It wasn't erotic, it wasn't transcendental, it certainly wasn't 'orgasmic', it was usually just sticky.

The smell and chilly feel of semen puddling in my knickers was the only evidence of what I had done, but it was difficult to ignore. Sometimes that trickling sensation was like a secret trophy, a reminder that I was now a sexual initiate, with a growing number of conquests under my belt; more often it was just irritating and scummy.

Cutting Up Playgirl

* * * *

Last night, after re-reading the above paragraphs, I went to bed, leaving my husband downstairs at his computer as usual. As I undressed I thought that I would try to remember what sex had been like, back in those days. So I got into bed and lay, instinctively, on my back, very still and straight, my arms wrapped around my breasts. I tried to find some real memories of that ancient sex, from the time when intercourse just felt like part of the job of being young. It was hard to stop the pursuit of memory being overtaken by imagination, which can always supply a picture, but I really wanted some authentic residue of how it had been.

I remembered cold lino under my feet and the misery of not being able to clean my teeth if I stayed the night in someone else's room. The identifying traces of different boys flashed up: a lip curling with the effort of maintaining cynicism, a pair of feet turned coyly inwards, a crowing hoot of laughter, a desperate need for nicotine. None of them really stood out sexually and, above all, what came back to me was the sheer perfunctoriness of the sex. Maybe I was a deadly cold fish, inhibiting the natural expressivity of these otherwise imaginative young men? I think the truer picture is that they were just as hung up about sex as I was; none of us was at ease with either our own bodies or those of the opposite sex. As far as I could remember, no student hands ever explored inside me, let alone tongues. It was a time when sexual technique was not the subject of countless ladmag features and my partners were drawn from a very specific subset of clever, middle-class white boys — all of which made for a repeating pattern of clinically disengaged coupling. As I dozed off, my efforts to drag up ancient memories of college sex left

Carrie Jones

me feeling oddly dissociated, unreal, and that was maybe the most authentic memory of all.

In those first few years, the best thing about sex for me was the discovery that people wanted to sleep with me. Sex was a currency of power rather than a source of pleasure – not anything as crude as a bargaining chip, but a fillip for me every time somebody wanted me and I acquiesced. To be chosen was to be worth something. But I soon realised that the exchange rate mechanism of this particular economy was more complicated than had originally seemed to be the case: the triumph of being 'The One' could soon be undermined by doubts about the position of the particular boy whose 'One' you were in the pop chart of sexual standing. My trouble was that I just couldn't resist telling my girlfriends about new conquests the next day – whatever had happened just didn't seem *credible* until I had dramatised it for my friends. I just loved the feeling of their attention focused on me as I made them laugh. A crude form of stand-up comedy, maybe, but I got a truer thrill from the *telling* than I did from the sex itself.

The thrill came with a risk, though – that, as I told them everything, I would see a look in my friends' eyes that it was hard not to interpret as surprise, or, worse, *pity*. It was much rarer to see envy. Perhaps this was down to my eccentric taste in boys or (as I prefer to think) because there were just so many boys to choose from in that swarming pool – we rarely lowered our hooks in front of the same fish. I can only think of one instance at college when three of us lusted after the same boy. It was quite a major crush on my part, as they always were. The boy, Phil, seemed highly desirable to me: funny, clever, and with a particular elasticity to his features which I found very attractive. The three of us enjoyed playing up our swooning whenever we'd seen Phil, but in the end it was me who got to spend the night with him.

How I was punished for besting my best friends! Phil was a white, middle-class brainbox just like all the others, and, I think, just as hung up, but he expressed his sexual anxiety in a markedly different way which came as a horrible shock. Sex with Phil was an encounter with a crazy lizard. Muttering and laughing to himself, thrashing and jerking his body, nipping and biting, he was truly scary. Staring at the ceiling afterwards, too spooked to sleep, I wondered what on earth I was doing, exposing myself physically and emotionally to the unpredictable strangeness of other humans who I barely knew. Without question it was the worst sex I've ever had, and I wonder now why on earth I went through with it and didn't just call a halt to the horror. In fact I even remember *smiling* at him, while I was undergoing his torture, thinking not that I must 'keep him sweet' but, much worse than that, that I must maintain the pretence of delight at being treated to the privilege of sex with him and on no account offend him by revealing my dismay. Still, daylight came, I got up and it was over. And it made a good story to tell the other two when I saw them later.

The other advantage of 'telling' was that it put the distance of narrative between me and the 'dirty' thing I had done. It was, in essence, a betrayal of the intimacy I *thought* I wanted, a way of escaping the scary marshlands of true intimacy. Throughout my life, if I have had to wish for something, or write down my ultimate desire, however trivial the occasion – I was once persuaded to place just such a secret wish inside a cardboard 'magic pyramid' whose owner urged me to believe the wish would come true – I have almost always wished for 'intimacy'. But now that I have had so many opportunities for it and have always, somehow, found a way to escape from it, I think that must be my *anti-wish*, the actual opposite of what my subconscious wants.

So many crushes. I have the most long-lived crushes, multiple crushes, and they don't die but persist while other 'live' relationships run their course, resurfacing undiminished on the other side. Crushes are fictions, just as Col from the concert was, gorgeously two-dimensional, man-shaped screens on which you can project all your sunny fantasies about them.

On my first day of college I got a crush on a blond-haired, kitten-faced student who was giving the new students a pep talk on 'joining in'. My instant devotion to him made me volunteer to staple together and distribute the college newsletter, of which he was the editor. As I went up to the front to 'sign up' I felt as though I was going up the aisle of a church to be married – surely everyone must see the magical aura of love dancing around me? Kitten-Face was a very popular boy; energetic and into sociable sports, he got things done. He wasn't interested in me beyond my ability to wield a stapler and type. I never really understood that the love-object might actually be aware that they were adored, be uncomfortable about it, and even limit their contact with me as a result.

About five years later, after I'd graduated, I met him again at a party. After all those years of adoration I had become quite good friends with K-F, but the crush I had on him had kept us permanently on terms akin to a vicar and a timid parishioner who hopes her flower-arrangements in the church will get her noticed. As the party wound up, K-F said, 'Oh, *come on* then,' as if to be finally done with an irritation. The shameful thing is that I *did* spend the night with him. The awful hollowness of affectless sex ensured that the crush was laid to rest.

There was another boy in my college who I thought was beautiful and charming and witty, and if he ever came to eat his lunch at the same table as me I would quietly fall apart. This happened once when I was eating cheese and biscuits and I can remember that the crackers began to explode in my fingers, crumbs shooting into the air like shrapnel. Other people on the table knew of my crush and laughed but I didn't mind because at least it was some sort of public acknowledgement of my passion. On another occasion I left my work spread out in the college library while I went to get a coffee, and when I came back this same boy, who was working nearby, had scribbled a comment on the page of notes I had left on the desk: 'Aha, "ironic", are you sure you don't mean sarcastic, or cynical? Is this ironic consciousness defeated by intransitive affirmation or does it lead to other possible modes of existence?' He was a Philosophy student, you see, and this was a Philosophy joke. It might not seem very sexy, but I was silly with pleasure. I loved the idea that he had come over to my things while I was gone, looked at them, and then left a sign that confessed to this moment of snooping. Of course I've kept the sheet of paper, but it doesn't do to look at it too often, because really the amount of thrillingness to be wrung out of it is limited. But still.

For all my interest in *The Story of O* and the Marquis de Sade, in spite of my persistent fantasies about complicated knots of copulating people, my secret excitement whenever I read accounts of French *échangiste* clubs, the most transgressive sexual act of my whole life was an 'orgy' that a friend and I indulged in in 1982. Having read Catherine Millet's accounts of orgies involving hundreds of nameless, faceless men, I realise that this episode barely deserves the name, but that's how we talked about it when we were excitedly psyching ourselves up for it. The 'orgy' consisted of her having sex (once) with a boy in the same room at the same time as I had sex (once) with another boy. The only other excitement was that we did it on the carpet! The two boys were in the year below us and seemed rather bruised by the experience. It was definitely a case of *us* choosing *them* to undergo 'thrills'. When it was over – and it was over *very* quickly – they looked very young and, somehow, *used*. There was a lot of giggling and then it was never mentioned again.

I am fascinated by the idea of crossing from 'ordinary' life into the world of transgression. How do people make the step across? What is it in their psychological make-up that enables some people to do it, and what is it in mine that forbids it? Would sex be any better if I did cross the line? I'm fascinated by any glimpse I get of those who *have* broken out of convention and are living a life of what can sometimes seem a kind of magical freedom. Yet I've noticed that 'ordinariness' seems to persist, even when people *have* 'crossed the line' and that's weirder still.

While I was at university and still heavily involved in 'women's issues', I once went with my friends to a lesbian disco, to 'show solidarity'. (What a lie! I was just being a terrible voyeur.) I don't mean to imply that it's not perfectly ordinary to be a lesbian, but for me the idea that I might have any gay aspects to my sexuality was in the same category as admitting I was curious about sado-masochism or bondage – witness my denial that kissing Caroline G had any lesbian overtones. Inside the disco, I was really taken aback to discover that most of the women were in couples which mimicked the most conventional kind of heterosexuality: the 'female' halves were in flowery, knee-length polyester dresses, the 'male' halves wore trousers and shirts with the occasional tweed cap. And just recently I saw a man on one of those find-me-a-lover makeover shows on television who admitted to having been a 'swinger', big time. Yet he was a preternaturally ordinary 'bloke', with jug ears and sticking-out teeth. The thought of *him* coming on all foxy over the bowl of car keys is something I would do well to bear in mind when I am restlessly wondering what it would be like to *try something different*.

As the years have accumulated, there *have* been one or two other episodes when I've edged closer to the kind of sex which is not plain, vanilla-flavoured and placidly unexciting. In truth I'm very curious about sex in all its baroque variations but I find it impossible to be open about it.

Once a boyfriend who was much older than me took me to Amsterdam for the weekend. We went with another couple who were also a decade or so older than me – 'grown ups' who enabled me to indulge the feeling that I was a passive little girl. Saturday night saw the others ordering a platter of oysters, proof of their sophisticated tastes. By the time I had steeled myself to tip a single cold, snot-like oyster down my throat they had emptied the dish, so I was spared having to eat any more. Then we walked up and down the city's pulsing corridors of neon and finally paid to go into a live sex show. It was my role as the 'child' in this group that enabled me to go along with the adult naughtiness. I was delighted to have been taken into the show and intensely curious as to what I would see.

It didn't last too long. First up was a pale, closed-up-looking girl who joylessly pleasured herself on stage for a few minutes. Then another whey-faced girl joined her and they boredly writhed against each other, kissing with all the passion of dolls pressed together by a child. Both were wearing thin evening gloves up to their elbows and I imagined these might hide the track marks of drug addiction – although they may simply have been intended to enhance their sexual allure.

The third act saw a thin man emerge onto the stage and have highly choreographed sex with the first girl whilst the second hovered like an anxious parlourmaid. Perhaps they were unemployed East European ballet dancers who had given up hopes of dancing in *Giselle* or *Swan Lake* and instead had brought their anaemic bodies to Amsterdam in an effort to make ends meet. This was *trabi*-sex, low-cost, low-energy, grey, dry, sad sex. But still, I was watching people *doing it*. I was pleased to have got in to the theatre, but it was impossible to feel titillated, and I found myself much more interested in imagining the circumstances of the performers. For me, this is almost always a by-product of pornography – a fascination with the settings in which it takes place and a curiosity about the stories that have brought the participants to this way of making a living.

Finally, climactically, a member of the audience was invited onto the stage to have sex with one of the girls. I was surprised they would allow such an interaction, thinking that these impromptu performers might not be able to control and de-energise their performances to the requisite degree. A grinning, swaggering, gesticulating sailor bounded onto the stage, unzipped himself, and, twisting back towards his mates in order to gloat at his good fortune, got to work on the thin girl. In the end, he turned out not to be such a loose cannon, but simply became one of the performers, consumed and judged by the audience: a bit spotty, not very big. We had paid for him, just as we'd paid for the others.

I found it fascinating to observe that sailor as he volunteered to perform sex in public. The apparent nonchalance with which he joined in with the performance epitomised my idea of transgression, and I wanted to study him to see if I could discover the secret which enabled him to transgress whilst I am so utterly incapable of it. To many people it might seem odd to aspire to the freedom to fuck in front of other people, but to me it seems that those who *dare* are somehow *their own person*. They feel they need account for their behaviour to no one but themselves. I, on the other hand, have not been able to break the hidden taboos that bind me to my parents and to other people who now symbolise parental authority, such as my husband. The pretence continues that I'm a good little girl and so I'm bound by a deep fear of discovery, that people will see just how *bad* I am inside.

A while ago I had to test my new inkjet printer so I did a squiggle on a page on my screen for it to print out. The squiggle was nothing, just a random wavy line done in half a second, but it happened to be in the shape of that classic graffito, a cock and balls. Before I had a chance to delete it, my husband came into the room and saw it. He hadn't even commented on it before I found myself furiously sobbing and shouting, hating him for seeing a flash of my subconscious, hating myself for letting a stupid doodle expose my fetid underside. My reaction was so over the top that it took even me by surprise – let alone my husband, who nonetheless failed to make light of the incident and thus only intensified my feelings of shame.

Yet here I am, writing it all down for a book, for public consumption. Do I have any idea how I'm going to handle that? And why is this impulse for self-exposure so strong when it contradicts so much that I know about myself?

Chapter 10

NO PARIS HILTON

So you weren't in Paris. I was very disappointed. Carrie, I thought about you so much as we turned the Polish soil.
Letter to me from Sean, September 1981 (age 19)

I thought I had been terribly smart to rent a pied-à-terre in Paris belonging to one of the French lecturers at the University for the summer holidays at the end of my first year. I had spotted the card advertising it on the faculty noticeboard and I assumed, because of its owner, that it would be elegant and comfortable. I had visions of a brilliant white room, flooded with light, with colourful abstract art on the walls. I had intended to take only my mother with me (it would be a good few years before I broke the habit of taking holidays with her), but the image of the beautiful Rive Gauche apartment belonging to the Cambridge professor was so powerful that it also seduced my father who, for the first time in our lives, decided to come on holiday with us.

This was a dreadful idea. It was so long since he had been abroad that, as soon as we had crossed the Channel, he was traumatised by every tiny deviation from the English norm – the upholstery on the train seats, the dryness of bread, the price of coffee, the ebullience of children. By the time we entered the Paris Metro for the last leg of our journey to Saint Germain des Près, he was tight-lipped with shock and Mum was so jittery with the effort of not irritating him further that she lost her ticket. This pathetic misdemeanour brought about the crisis towards which the whole journey had been building: me snapping at her in exasperation, her almost in tears, him silently enraged and full of hate. But the brilliant white apartment, our haven, the cool balm to soothe all our tensions, was now only a few streets away. We made our way in a straggling column to the rue de Seine, the incredible cartographic knowledge of Paris I had gained during my stint as an au pair coming in handy at last.

The apartment block was just too Parisian for words. The door was a massive bulwark with a tiny slot cut in it, through which we had to clamber. A sour-faced concièrge straight out of a Balzac novel gave us the keys and gesticulated rudely towards the stairs.

'Troisième.'

It was the exhausted mouse desperately trying to fling itself up the staircase that gave us the first clue as to the true nature of our luxury accommodation. Then the stench of the communal lavatories on each landing forced us to face reality a little more squarely with each flight of stairs we climbed. We eventually opened the door onto a one-room hovel furnished with splintering crates and dirty foam-rubber blocks. I was horribly disappointed, and ashamed to have brought my parents to this slum. But if I was disappointed, my father was almost extinguished by betrayal and alienation. He seemed bewildered, bludgeoned into submission, hating everything but bearing it with the numbed acceptance of a refugee.

Every minute that we spent in the apartment was awkward, with embarrassment, discomfort, shame and hostility bobbing about between us like barrage balloons. The only small relief was that we didn't have to use the communal loo because the flat had a tiny bathroom built into one corner. Otherwise, it was a question of avoiding each other's eyes as we shuffled about the wretched room. It was very hot and we opened the large windows overlooking the internal courtyard, whose walls were streaked with filth (one thought, inevitably, of chamberpots). Along with a whisper of cooler air came the sounds and smells of grubby life in all the other apartments.

Night time was the worst, when there was nothing for it but to lie down together on the crumbling squares of foam rubber. My father would not lie anywhere near my mother, and I didn't want to be near him, so the awkwardness built to a critical pitch. Then, when we were all lying miserably awake in the hot darkness, the sounds of people having sex would begin to rise up from other apartments and invade our room. I wished myself dead, and I meant it.

By day, there were Dutch boys in the apartment opposite who catcalled and threw coins through our windows. Instead of being outraged by this, or amused, or even flattered, I was mortified, choosing to interpret it in the most self-punishing way – obviously they had somehow seen through me and realised that I was nothing better than a whore.

In our billet, all was suffering and tense, accusatory silence. It may sound like nothing more than a dreadful holiday disaster but in fact it was just an intensified version of the way things always were. In the restricted space of the flat, the taut lines of inescapable relatedness cut into us. The dead weight of failed love pulled them deeper into our flesh. We all felt it. We were all oppressed by it. It was impossible to be cheerful about anything while we were so conscious of our misery, even though it was never referred to in words.

We tried going out to a restaurant. On his trip to collect me from my au-pairing stint, my father had been full of bile when the Berthauds took him out for *pizza* instead of the rich bouillabaisse or cassoulet he had dreamed of — surely it would lift the gloom if he could finally enjoy the classic French meals of his imagination? The ploy didn't work: the strain was only worsened by his refusal to pay the prices at even the most unambitious and uninviting restaurants. Good value for him would have been prices not seen since apple-cheeked *mesdemoiselles* welcomed the Americans with a kiss as they liberated Paris at the end of World War Two. Even the cheapest *menu à prix fixe* (consisting of, say, shrivelled radishes, fibrous horse steak and the inevitable crème caramel) offended him with its outrageously inflated price. A cup of coffee at a pavement café sent him into a sneering rage of resentment. He has an extraordinary capacity to be personally offended by the most commonplace realities. But when a drunken madwoman lurched crazily into our table, seized his cup of overpriced coffee and, muttering lugubriously to herself, drained it, he was thrilled. Referring to her as *La Goulue*, after a tarnished prostitute in a painting by Toulouse-Lautrec, he talked excitedly about her and, the next day, went out on his own to see if he could spot her again. It seemed that, for my father, she held the promise of some more authentic version of Paris. She was a cipher for all the great novels and paintings set in the city, Paris *imaginaire*, populated by the insane and the louche.

Unable to sleep, my father took to getting up in the early hours of the dawn and slipping out into the streets to observe the prostitutes and other misfits, the drunks on all-nighters, the tramps. Anxiety about what he would get up to on these escapades mingled with relief in the sad little room after he'd gone, as my mother and I finally dozed off.

The days were little better. Even as we suffered, we went through the motions of being ordinary tourists, but this façade was paper-thin and easily punctured. When my father dropped his cigarette lighter (a cherished leaving present) down a drain in the Jardin de Luxembourg, a fresh spike of angst stabbed above the level we were already enduring. The three of us stood around the drain cover, staring down at the lighter gleaming in the dried leaves below, my father softly moaning swear words like a fallen nun giving birth. Peter Sellers would have been perfect to play my dad in the film of these abysmal days: he would have captured the pained rage my father seemed to feel constantly, at himself, at me and my mother, at the world; he would have been able to express Dad's mixture of defeat and resistance; he would have known how to be both aggressor and victim in just the way my dad did.

The lighter was retrieved by a kindly park attendant.

On another day we took the train to Versailles and walked drearily about the gardens. When we reached the meadows of the Trianon, Dad took off his shoes, placed them neatly together under a tree, and lay down with his head resting on them. It was hard to imagine Marie Antoinette tripping about with her shepherdess's crook and perfumed sheep when all we could see was my father's pale-white toe sticking out of his sock and his cheeks sunken with fatigue and unhappiness. The sight of his martyr's head resting on his dusty shoes was both pitiful and offensive. My mother and I went off to do the tour of the house and were able to find a little relief laughing and complaining about him once we were out of earshot.

After six unremitting days, Dad decided to go home. Without him, the shoddy apartment began to seem almost homely. We managed not to think too much about his lonely journey home, still dazed from his grim experiences, like an ox that has only been stunned by the blow that was intended to kill it.

For the next few days we walked arm in arm around the Latin Quarter, read our books on the steps of Saint Sulpice, saw *The Elephant Man* and Bette Midler's *The Rose* at the local cinema, window-shopped down the Boulevard Saint Germain and raked up and down the terraces of graves in Père Lachaise. We were like lovers in our happy self-containment. But it was starting to prey on my mind that Sean had said he might call in to stay with us for a few days, on his way back from a whistle-stop tour of the socialist hotspots of Europe. This plan dated from the distant time when the apartment had only existed as a Platonic ideal of airy sophistication. The thought of Sean arriving at the apartment, of him seeing the firewood furniture and the dirty mattresses, of him *sleeping* there, with *me*, and *my mum*, and the Dutch boys, sent me into more and more of a panic. (Of course, being so *radical*, he would probably have taken the squalor in his stride, might even have approved of it, but I wasn't seeing it from *his* point of view.) As ever when I couldn't deal with boys, I had the urge to run away. We had rented the apartment for the whole of August, but I started to worry away at my mother about wanting to go home. I don't remember quite how I persuaded her that we had to go home – but I do know I never mentioned her rival, Sean. Just as we were leaving the apartment to make our way to the Gare du Nord, I told Mum I was going to have a last check around the flat and, as she set off down the smelly staircase for the last time, I pinned a note for Sean on the door, saying that we had had to leave unexpectedly.

A few days after we got home, rejoining my father (now restored to more or less normal levels of sourness), a letter arrived with a French stamp. It was from Sean, a sighing note of regret. He had arrived at the rue de Seine apartment only a day after we had left and had found my note pinned to the door.

There was a certain Romantic poignancy in his having missed us by so narrow a margin. I congratulated myself on a finely judged escape.

Chapter 11

TWITCHING IN CAMBRIDGE

In erotic relationships dominated by the Imaginary, each love will attempt to capture their own image in the other.
Notes on 'Lacanian basics' in a notebook from 1983 (age 20)

ONE of my most treasured photos shows a tall boy with curly hair and glasses. He's wearing moleskin trousers and a pair of pristine Converse All-Stars. He's taking the picture himself with a button on the end of a wire and he's looking away to the side of the frame. Even though he must have posed for the picture because he chose the moment when the shutter was released, he manages to look very natural, leaning against the scuffed white wall of the student house where I had two ground-floor rooms. The boy's name was Robin Singer, and by the time this photograph was taken I had become quite close to him. Most of our friends probably thought of us as boyfriend and girlfriend and in a strangely formal way we were. But, then again, we weren't.

A few months before the photo, on a memorably crisp winter morning, I had been crossing the beautiful, intimate court at the heart of my college when I met Robin coming in the other direction with a friend. They were in the year above and reading English, so at least two notches superior to me. I already admired Robin because he played in a band, a serious electro-pop band in the mould of very early Simple Minds – all repetitive synth tracks and growly foreboding.

Carrie Jones

Robin stopped. 'Hi. I've been meaning to ask you. Would you like to swap jackets?'

I looked down at what I was wearing. It was a zip-up jacket made of pale pink-and-white-striped seersucker, rather thin for the cold bright weather, but I had bought it in France at the end of my year as an au pair and I was very fond of it.

'*This* jacket?'

'Yeah. And you can have my leather one.'

I should have had my suspicions there and then, but this was the early Eighties and the New Romantics had played havoc with gender markers. Besides, I was hugely flattered. Robin Singer liked my jacket. Liked me, perhaps! I unzipped the jacket and tugged my hands through the elasticated cuffs. And Robin put it on, still warm from my body.

'Great, thanks. Come round and get the leather one off me.'

So that's how it began.

I went to Robin's rooms that afternoon. He had a two-room 'set' in the oldest, nicest part of the college. His sitting-room was immaculately tidy, and he had somehow purged it of most of the ugly college furniture. How he had done this was quite unfathomable. There was a wonderful painting on the wall, perhaps a Ben Nicholson abstract, borrowed from Kettle's Yard, the art-filled house in Cambridge which I loved. Some appealingly thunky music was bupping away in the background as Robin made a pot of tea. I remember trying to condense my body into the smallest possible space as I sat on the sofa: it seemed wrong to take up too much room, or, worse, to have loose ends – arms, legs – flying about, messing things up. I wanted to be self-contained in that neat room where everything was so deliberately placed.

I was in awe of Robin, but I made a huge effort to disguise the signs of my intensifying adulation and to project some sort of 'cool' version of myself. After all, he had wanted *my* jacket, hadn't he? *My* pink jacket. (In fact he was still wearing the jacket that afternoon, his thin wrists poking just a little too far out of the tight cuffs.) And I was easily able to hold my own on the music front. The John Peel Years had been a magnificent training ground and I was now able to talk impressively about virtually any alternative pop topic from The Adverts to ZTT. So we sat and drank tea and then Robin noodled around on his synthesizer for a bit and showed me his eight-track recording system. I was impressed. Before we knew it, it was time for dinner and I asked Robin if he was going down to eat in the college refectory.

'Oh no, no, I never eat down there. I just eat in here. I only like bread and cheese and ham and stuff. You can eat with me, if you like.'

So the perfection continued and I stayed to eat Robin's lovely neat, precise food, taking exceptional care not to drop crumbs or spill my water. I loved the way that Robin seemed to be taking such care with his existence, the way that everything was just so. Most students seemed to be willing victims of entropy, but Robin had entropy neatly folded away in a drawer.

When I reluctantly felt I should go, Robin suggested we meet up later to watch *Top of the Pops*. And so the defining ritual of our relationship was initiated. The college didn't encourage its students to watch television. There was no comfortable TV lounge, but if you were really desperate you were allowed to go into the kitchen staff's rest room where there was a small television. You did have to be desperate, because a trip to this room was enough to put you off college food for ever. (Perhaps this was the straightforward explanation for Robin's avoidance of the refectory?) First you walked through the elegant portico of the college chapel, a high, curvaceous arch – but this was a deceptive entry-point for you immediately found yourself in a narrow alley running down towards the river, a stinking ginnel which never featured in the guided tours. At the very end, past the overflowing wheelie bins, past the open doors of the kitchens and the sound of unfamiliar Cambridge accents shouting and joking, past the staff lavatory with its hopeful sticker, 'Now Wash Your Hands', was a room, built in the Sixties, which overhung the river Cam. No member of the kitchen staff was ever using the room when we went down there, but it was always littered with plates greedily overfilled with college food and barely touched. Half glasses of beer were lined up like skittles. The windows permanently left open to dispel the smell of stale beer, you could see the tops of punt poles lurching past and hear the giggles of hopeful girls being romanced by hoorays.

So, that night, at half past seven, I went down the alley to the TV room for the first time, pulling a face at the smells, the *awful* smells, and imagining I saw a rat behind the bins. When I arrived, Robin was sitting in a Sixties armchair which must have dated from the room's first pristine days, but which was now decorated with an ormolu of shiny chewing gum. The lights were off and Robin's face was animated by the flashing disco lights on the screen. The first band were playing – was it The Jam with 'Town Called Malice'? Or OMD with 'Souvenir'? Neither would have been quite what Robin and I liked (I had *no* intention of confessing that I had once been in the Orchestral Manouevres in the Dark fanclub), but at least those records were on 'our side' of the divide which we perceived between acceptable and unbearable music. I sat down in the armchair next to Robin. His arm lay along the varnished wooden arm of his chair; my arm lay parallel along mine. At some point, without seeming to move, Robin put his hand over mine and that was it, the declaration of our interest in each other and, more or less, the consummation of it.

I cherished the evenings we subsequently spent watching television together in that fetid room, and well I might, because that was about as good as it got. When we walked back up the side of the college and out into the court, Robin would kiss me on the cheek and we would go our separate ways. That kiss was strange, eloquent... If I hadn't been so besotted with him I would perhaps have analysed it more closely. It was a ritualistic kiss, always the same. He would smile theatrically, his lips twitching. His body would stiffen, lean away from me, hesitate, and then his head would dart in and the kiss would be bestowed. I didn't think about it at the time, I was just grateful for a sign of his affection, but really, anyone not blinded by love might perhaps have picked up on a degree of *reluctance*, even *distaste*, at this facial contact.

I wasn't in any doubt that Robin liked me. We got on so well together, our interests and enthusiasms chiming perfectly. And it must have been gratifying for him, at least at first, to have such a devoted acolyte, someone who tried so hard never to outstay her welcome and respected his need for time on his own, who shared his taste in music to the last semi-quaver, and who genuinely admired his work (not just his plinky-plinky synthesizer music: Robin was also very keen on photography and I used to pick his reject prints out of his waste-paper bin and keep them). I thought I was doing a fantastic job of *not* pushing Robin for more boyfriendly action. True, by the summer, his hand on my hand in the television room had progressed to *my* hand laid lightly on his *thigh*, but I felt almost ethereal from the months of saintly abstention.

Robin's not wanting sex immediately came as a relief after

Sean's (very normal) sexual appetite. With Sean sex had seemed utterly straightforward, neatly integrated into our lives as a committed leftwing couple. Sexual politics was a major plank of the Left then and it was necessary to have one's relationship running in an acceptable way – in theory a very good thing for women but in practice tending to render sex a little joyless, if respectful. The deal for the right-on man was that you made sure you were not a *sexist pig* and in return you got masses of polite, non-exploitative sex. So, you learnt to refer to the sex organs by their non-derogatory names and you were away. I had participated in the non-sexist sex in the spirit of a young nun who gladly gets up at four in the morning to kneel in silent prayer on cold flagstones: in her zeal for the life she has chosen, she transcends personal discomfort. She does not question the validity of the rules to which her life is now subject. She does not expect 'fun'. So it was with me. When Robin followed Sean in the sequence of my boyfriends, it seemed delightful not to be expected to return immediately to the dignity of sexual labour.

It was too early in my sex life for me to have gained any sort of perspective or to be able to compare what I was 'getting' with what might conceivably be on offer. I was just *in it*. But I idolised Robin and that meant he could do no wrong.

Robin was taking his finals and, in a very Robin-like way, had won a dispensation from the University to sit his exams alone in a small room, presumably because being forced to rub gowns with the other students might have brought on some debilitating phobia. On the morning of his first exam – and in spite of my own examinations being imminent – I got up at around six and set off on my stunted bicycle to gather flowers from the water meadows to make a good-luck bouquet for him. At the time it seemed the most romantic idea I had ever had.

Unfortunately, the water meadows of Cambridge, quite counter to my expectations, offered up a Saharan paucity of pretty species. On I went, along the riverbank, past the early morning rowers, my eyes searching for splashes of colour. I cycled far beyond the familiar tight streets of the city centre until outlying districts began to meet up in ways I hadn't previously understood. At one point I found myself on a multi-laned flyover that I hadn't even known existed. I pressed on to Grantchester, haunt of Rupert Brooke and Jeffrey Archer – surely there would be flowers *there*? But no, only pungent ragwort and thistles. Things were getting desperate. The sun was blazing overhead now. Soon it would be too late. I wanted Robin to find the flowers when he left his room to go to the exam. I got off my bike and scuttled around in the long grass, bent double. In the end I found a few buttercups and milkweeds, a couple of drooping poppies and finally added in some snapdragons which were sprouting on the pavement near my digs. I cycled round to college and left the pathetic bunch outside Robin's room. I do not believe any mention was ever made of them.

I really couldn't say where I was with Robin, though we were definitely connected in some tenuous way. When we visited Kettle's Yard house together and sat on the long, white sofa there, holding hands, I felt tremendously happy and privileged to be there with him. He took such care with everything in his life, it was impossible not to feel proud that he had, in some unspecified way, chosen me.

But it was not straightforward. He told me that the previous summer in Portugal he had been seriously in love with someone, a Portuguese woman. For a long time he was reluctant even to tell me her name, and when he did it sounded to me like a Moorish incantation. The implication was that he was still bound by her spell, unable to love another. I thought I could bear anything, just to be allowed to spend time with Robin. I liked him so much that anything was better than nothing, and I really thought I was achieving a kind of emotional detachment and forgetting about the sex which everyone else was enjoying in profligate quantities.

It seems I was wrong. In spite of my efforts, poor Robin felt horribly pressured. He felt bad that his little sidekick, his Batgirl, wasn't getting the intimacy she so desperately and obviously craved. One afternoon he arrived at my rooms unexpectedly while I was studying. He was doing the twitching smile.

'I thought we could, you know…' His voice trailed off. His eyebrows gestured weakly towards my bedroom, behind him.

I used to spend nearly every afternoon dozing off and jerking awake over the massive French and Italian novels I had to plough through. I was notorious for sleeping at my desk. I was convinced the gas fire was slowly asphyxiating me. I blinked at him and breathed in a deeper lungful of carbon monoxide in an effort to wake up.

'What, *now*? Oh, right, okay, *yes*.' *Gift horses and all that.*

Putting down my book, I stood up and came over to where Robin was standing. He put his arms gingerly round me and we kissed, less chastely than we had ever kissed before – there was actual lip-on-lip contact, but I feel certain the thought of *bacteria* crossed his mind. Yet something had made him determined to do right by me.

Naturally there was no tearing of clothes or any other signifier of frantic passion. In an orderly manner, we went into my bedroom which had a separate door along a little gloomy corridor.

Robin left his shoes outside the door, and for some reason this made me think of his Portuguese woman, that perhaps she had insisted on the removal of shoes in her *casa*.

My bedroom was at the back of the house, where it was dug into a hill. A mound of earth obscured the sunlight and left the room permanently cold. We took off our clothes and climbed primly into the single bed. My body, united, at last, with Robin's, generated no heat to take the edge off the chill air. All I could think of was the need to keep my cold feet away from him, as if they were shameful. We lay next to each other and kissed with all the warmth of a classical sculpture. It was surprisingly hard to go from translation to penetration with no preamble. I adored Robin, I really did, but it had become obvious he was nursing some major hang-up about sex. I didn't want to scare him away, now that he had come to me like this. It was like feeding a little birdy: I felt I should keep really still until he took what I was offering him. Very delicately, and with some slightly disconcerting 'mmm' sounds, which *might* have indicated a certain pleasure, but which might just as easily have been the beginnings of full-blown retching, Robin levered himself on top of me and, taking great care to make no sudden movements, I let him enter me. *Milli*seconds later, he was sitting on the edge of the bed saying that he felt sick – sick and dizzy. He hung his head low and closed his eyes. I patted him nervously on the back. Was it the sudden rush of blood away from his brain? Or the nausea of visceral revulsion?

Suddenly there was noise outside the door – first of all a tap at my sitting-room door, then a lot of muffled sniggering and what sounded like people who were helpless with laughter marshmallowing into each other.

Then the hammering of jackbooted Nazis on the bedroom door.

'Carrie! We know you're in there!' A lot more sniggering.
The *shoes*.

Robin seemed to shimmer into ectoplasm, to will himself to nothingness. We sat in wretchedness for what seemed like forever until the sniggerers started to sound tetchy and finally left without their quarry.

You'd think that such a dismal coupling would have put paid to our relationship, but I was nothing if not kind. And a bit desperate. I had already invested a great deal in my relationship with him amongst my female friends – declaring my love for him, bragging about his superior lifestyle and so on. I was in too deep to ship out now. Besides, the whole episode was already taking on an almost mystical quality: he was obviously just too pure for the scuzziness of sex. Besides, his band was booked to play at one of the May Balls and I was due to go with them and be a hanger-on. I didn't want to miss that

But, a couple of days before the Ball, I found a note in my pigeonhole. Robin had gone away, to the remote parts of Scotland. He had run away from me. Once he had got away, he didn't stop running. I had quite a few very pleasant letters and cards from him, each one from further away. Finally, eight months later, a letter arrived from the other side of the world in which, at last, Robin tried to talk about 'us'. In very carefully considered, elegant sentences, he said that he was 'not a person to fall in love with' because he had 'no desire to be loved'. (Actually, that last bit was crossed out, but only very delicately, so that it could still be easily read.)

Robin's sexual elusiveness definitely intensified his appeal for me, preserving him in the aspic of aloofness. If I had been fully involved with him, I am certain my unrealistically perfect image of him would have become fogged and spoiled – that's what has happened with everyone else I have got to know too well.

These days, it sometimes amuses me to put Robin's name into Google to see what comes up (it's no good you trying this, reader, because I've changed his name…), for Robin has become something of a minor recording star, a big fish in a small pondy subsection of the music business, and I like to see if any new photographs of him have been posted, or any fresh fawning interviews transcribed. He doesn't look half as good to me in his current incarnation as he does in my photo of him leaning against the wall in Cambridge. I'm glad I've got that.

Chapter 12

ROME EXPRESS

He is very sweet and charming. He paints and is really interested in Italian art. He has been showing me round all the Baroque villas and churches ... It is very civilised.

Letter home from Rome, 21 July 1982 (age 20)

MAYBE I was just on the rebound, or maybe I was more badly affected by sexual frustration than I had realised during the saintly months with Robin, but very shortly after he had taken the high road to Scotland I took the low road to enough sex to make up for the preceding dearth.

I wasn't too down about Robin's escape – at least it relieved the odd sense of guilt I had been feeling, the suspicion that he had regretted getting involved with me even while I was 'cherishing his specialness'. Even though I had sat on my hands instead of pawing him like a puppy as I longed to, I felt I had been too much for him. My adoration was a heavy burden to carry. *In absentia*, he could revert to iconic form in my memory and I built a little shrine to him there. (Shrine-building, I now see, is something I've done a great deal of.)

Then one evening I went to the pictures with a friend and a large group of her friends. I sat next to a boy I'd never met before, not fantastically good-looking but very present, very intense. He was notably tall, but even with this large frame, his head seemed to be built to a larger scale, and his nose to an even larger one. He was like a tricky exercise in perspective drawing.

There were hardly any seats left in the cinema and we all had to sit down in the front row with the movie roaring and thrashing right overhead, quite out of focus. I didn't even know this boy's name yet, but all during the film our legs touched, the near-unintentional pressure slyly developing into a wordless declaration of arousal.

I've read that you make a judgement about whether you want to sleep with someone within five seconds of setting eyes on them. Without being aware of it, I must have fancied this boy in the few moments before the lights went down. Otherwise I don't think I would have found my sedentary dance with him so erotic. Could I connect in this way with a *complete* stranger, someone I had not even set eyes on for a few seconds? It hasn't happened yet. There was a craze recently for dating in pitch darkness: strangers gather in a blacked-out restaurant; waiters in night-vision goggles serve tactile finger food (knives are considered too much of a risk) whilst you get to know your dining companions without seeing their features. By all accounts, inhibitions evaporate, flesh is sneakily palpated, and by the time the candles are lit for dessert, intense feelings have been unleashed, without the usual prejudgements based on physical appearance having interfered. (But what if the man you have flirted with so outrageously under the delicious cover of darkness turns out to be a fat-lipped toad who repels you? Would your synthetic arousal allow you to see beyond his amphibian looks, or would you just make your excuses and run?) Dating in the dark makes great fantasy material, but in reality I would rather be the one in the night-vision specs, voyeuristically seeing all.

When the cinema lights went up, I found out that the boy I

had rubbed thighs with was called Neil. He was keen on art, it turned out, and after we had come out of the pictures (our legs stiff from all that awkward invisible rubbing stuff), he took me to see an 'installation' he'd been working on. The attraction between us was so strong that we left our friends to be on our own together. We walked through the city centre to the back of a row of shops where he stopped in front of the sort of brick bay which usually houses a gigantic wheelie bin full of chicken gizzards but which, in this case, was empty except for a propped up scaffolding pole.

'There.' Neil gestured grandly towards the bay.

Peering at the ground in the darkness, I could just make out some faint chalk lines.

'Obviously it has more impact in daylight.'

Obviously. I nodded enthusiastically. Apparently the marks recorded where the shadow of the pole had fallen at various significant moments. You had to be there really.

I have always imagined that my ideal lover would be an artist and it was delightful to be madly fancied by someone for a change. When Neil invited me to go away to the Peak District that weekend, I agreed at once. I remember laughing about it with my friends, who dubbed Neil 'the axe murderer' in the face of this alarming willingness on my part to go off with him knowing little more about him than his name. Yet even as I was laughing I was thinking that maybe I should be a *little* bit careful, because you never knew. But sometimes you're just in the mood to grab at someone, simply because you can. For some people this might mean sex in a pub car park at closing time (and admittedly that *could* have a certain raw appeal), but in my case it meant, in the first instance, a weekend in the Peak District making charcoal sketches of fallen trees. It was just the start of a summer of previously unimaginable risk-taking and secrecy.

Of course Neil *wasn't* an axe murderer, but he was a little bit strange. Really it was just that I had never before encountered someone so pulsating with life. He was full of energy and plans and intense friendships. During our weekend away in the Peak District, when we weren't out sketching the trees, we went happily to bed together. *I* was happy, not self-conscious (that made a change), caught up in his verve.

I've noticed that I have a tendency to disbelieve things which don't coincide with my own experience of them. Thus, the very concept of sexual satisfaction sometimes seems bogus. The ceaseless cacophony of voices, in the media, in books, banging on about being utterly fulfilled by sex – it's reassuring to dismiss them as dishonest, colluding in a massive pretence. Admitting that maybe I am missing some necessary component for satisfaction, a psychological widget, is too frightening. With Neil, the memory of my attraction to him is easily accessible and I know, too, that I felt sexual *desire* for him. But the sex itself, the sexual connection, is not something I can drag up from memory, and I suspect that's because there was no connection. Luckily, Neil was unaware of the vacuum at the heart of me, as was I then. His gung-ho appetite for sex drowned out that awful silence within me. Neil was crazy about Italy, and had made plans to spend the summer in Rome. He'd already sorted out a room in a flat. He wanted me to go with him.

As I was due to spend the whole of the coming year in Italy, teaching English in a secondary school, it seemed positively sensible to go to Rome before my year out officially started, to try to improve my very poor Italian. Telling myself that I was doing the sensible thing was tremendously reassuring and quietened the voice in my head that advised a little more caution. Another voice whispered that it would be romantic, sexy, cool to go abroad with Neil. Sensible *and* sexy was a combination to defeat caution any day.

I went to Rome without telling my parents where I was going. I have no idea where they thought I was. It was the night of the Tom Robinson Band concert revisited – me crucified by the need to keep my 'adventures' secret, and them not actually being the slightest bit bothered. Or, if they were, hiding it exceptionally well.

My mother always says that she was left to her own devices from the age of four, so I expect she had been longing for me to get on with my life. I had just turned twenty, after all. But it was so much easier to slip away rather than formally acknowledge that I was an adult now. During my year as an au pair (when I had effectively left home) I had written in my diary, 'I can't reconcile myself to the fact that my childhood is over ... but I think once you've made the definitive split from your parents you can't, or mustn't, slip sneakily back into the cocoon. The step has been taken and others must be taken, faster and faster until you're at a run.' I like the picture this evokes of a joyful, whooping escape, but it just isn't borne out by the reality of my endless prim, self-censored letters home.

If I had been able to tell my parents that I was going to stay with a boyfriend in Rome, then the stay itself might have been less steeped in guilty feelings. As it was, I only told them where I was once I had arrived, and in my letter home I took care to paint a very bland picture of the highly sexual, hyperactive, twenty-four-hour man to whose care I had entrusted myself.

Neil came to meet me at Termini, the teeming central station in Rome. We caught a bus out to the suburbs and his flat. The city was overwhelming, even from a bus: huge, intensely alive, crammed with art — it was a Neil metaphor. Neil had already been there for a couple of weeks and he was keen to show me how he had already got under the city's skin — no mere tourist, he already had a network of friends here, and he had been visiting not only churches and *palazzi*, but cinemas, clubs, people's homes. The bus stormed across the huge Piazza Venezia, past the monument to Vittorio Emmanuele II. In a very few days' time I would be scurrying across this same square just like everyone else, scattering like insects in the paths of mad Roman drivers. Unlike everyone else, only I would have Neil manically shouting information at me as I ran: *that's* where Mussolini made his Fascist speeches, *that's* where we're meeting Paolo and Carmela tomorrow night, *that's* where the bus to Ostia leaves from. Through the bus window, I watched the massive ruins of ancient Rome move past like a frieze: the Forum, Trajan's Column, the Baths of Caracalla, all so solid and confident amongst the indifferent modern buildings. The red-brick ruins and the yellow stucco of the town houses gradually gave way to palm-lined suburban avenues and repetitive grids of white apartment blocks.

Neil scanned the passing streets intently. It was virtually impossible to see any distinguishing marks from one block to the next, but he suddenly jumped up and rang the bell for us to be let off. As the bus pulled swiftly away, we stood on the pavement with my suitcase. The ground-floor level of the nearest block of flats was given over to a little supermarket and a *pasticceria*. Outside the cake shop old men in black suits sat at aluminium tables waving flies away from their espressos and staring so intently at me with my suitcase and my wired boyfriend (was he really my *boyfriend*? I hadn't even considered the question properly yet) that I cast down my eyes in shame. I sensed their disapproval seeping into me, and I felt guilty of committing an outrage against their culture. For all they knew, I might be a very properly married young lady, or Neil's sister even, but I projected my guilty feelings onto them and they came zipping straight back at me from all those steely black eyes.

We went up to the tiny flat where Neil was staying, which was identical to so many other Italian flats I've been in with their cheap, dark furniture and ugly fittings. He was sharing it with another English boy but this boy was hardly ever there. When he did come back he too made clear his disapproval of my being there, but it was almost certainly on the grounds that I was an unofficial tenant and used the bathroom too much, rather than that I was a slut of a girl, sleeping with a man I barely knew.

Neil had already got his room arted up: huge, ragged charcoal drawings of twisted figures pressed in from the walls and postcards of Rinascimento paintings he'd already seen and loved were slipped into the window frames. I found a corner to shove my case into and sat down on the bed feeling untethered. Here I was in this room, in this apartment block, in this regimented density of suburban streets, in this country; yet I was nowhere. No one but Neil on the entire planet knew where I was. Nowhere and nobody.

I didn't even know Neil well enough to have got over the awkward stage — would he remember how I liked my tea? Had we even told each other our birthdays and middle names? Yet here he was, flopping down on the bed beside me, nuzzling at my lap, undoing my clothes. Come on, you weird creature, just for once say that you enjoyed sex, straightforwardly and happily. You fancied Neil and he fancied you and you had come a thousand miles to have happy sex with him and see a beautiful city.

That *is* how it was, for a while.

I couldn't help but be lifted up and carried along by Neil's incredible energy. I was a bug-eyed passenger hanging on to the running board as he careered all over the city and beyond. Recently I looked at a map of Rome to remind myself where we went and was astonished at the number of places which jumped out at me. We seem to have been everywhere: the Pantheon, Trastevere, the Pincio, to see all the great Renaissance statues and fountains, the Corso, the Spanish Steps, the Villa Doria Pamphili, the Roman Forum, covering the streets like orienteers collecting flags, all in the burning heat. Then I looked at a larger map and remembered trips we made outside the city, to Tivoli, the Villa d'Este and Ostia Antica. All of this activity was determined by Neil, steered by Neil. I went along with him, because he always knew more than me about everything, was always six or seven jumps ahead. I must have seemed like the ideal holiday companion, cheerfully falling in with whatever he had lined up, but quite soon my passivity began to have an insidious effect.

I was used to taking charge on journeys. From an early age I had insisted that my mother hand over railway tickets into my safekeeping, and I always took it upon myself to check on platform numbers and departure times. The very first time I flew abroad, when I was nine, I remember arriving at Luton airport for our package holiday to Greece and telling my mum to stay put whilst I set off across the immense white space to find our check-in desk. I had had to be in charge ever since we had been travelling back by train from visiting my great aunt in the Fens and had failed to get off at the right station for our connection. The sensation of the train rattling on through the night, unstoppably, with me wrongly inside it was so terrible. The more a situation makes me anxious, the more I try to take charge of it, so trotting after Neil, though to all appearances easy enough, went against the grain. Nothing ever went wrong and, what's more, left to myself I would never have arranged so many exciting outings, but I just couldn't quite trust him, because the only person I really trusted was myself.

One day we took a train heading north and, after about thirty miles, got out at the Lago di Bracciano. It's only by looking at a map now that I can write that sentence – at the time I had absolutely no idea what direction we were travelling in, or how far we had gone. The lake seemed as wide as a sea and the shoreline more like a beach, with white sand shelving gently down into clear shallow water. It was very quiet with no other people around. How did Neil know where to go? How did he know where we would get to when he waded into the water and began walking along the edge of the lake? I had no choice but to follow him – I had to trust him because I had no one else to turn to, but he seemed so foolhardy that I would have much preferred to let go of his coat tails and to sink down on the sand, crying with self-pity. Yet if I didn't stick with him, I felt I would be in danger – who might come along and scoop me up if I floundered in this alien place?

Where was my sense of adventure? My ability to have fun? In this context I was entirely lacking both. If I had been responsible for myself, I might have set out resolutely (with a comprehensive guidebook, of course, some worthy successor to Baedeker) to visit somewhere that was 'worth the effort'; staunch walking boots, a stout stick and a veil to keep insects away would have been my ghostly accessories. As it was, my exaggerated feebleness belonged more to my fearful child self than to the twenty-year-old I was now.

As we walked, the sandy strip would dwindle every so often

and the trees and reeds crowd down into the shallows, so we would be pushing aside willow branches and feeling mud between our toes instead of sand. I didn't like it. The sand I could 'read' with my feet, I could trust it, but the reeds and the mud were frightening, you couldn't see the bottom, even though the water was only a few inches deep. Then, slipping out from a reed bed, I saw a snake, black and slender, undulating through the water just in front of me. It seemed like a ribbon of water itself, differentiated from the surrounding liquid only by its inky colour. I had invaded its medium and I felt I shouldn't have been there. I was terrified. But I had no choice other than to stand still and let it slide past me.

Eventually we came to a village of low white houses clustered in by the lake. It was nearly dusk and, rather than finding our way back to the station, Neil suggested we stay the night – it would be romantic. Now that I was on asphalt again I felt a lot more cheerful, and we walked hand in hand through the village looking for a *pensione*. A sign outside a house advertised rooms so we knocked. An old lady came to the door and Neil talked to her in the Italian that he had picked up with enviable speed. We both smiled at her.

She narrowed her eyes at us. '*Siete sposi?*' Are you married?

'*Oh, sì, sì, signora.*'

The old woman hesitated, then stood back to allow us to enter. As I walked into the house behind Neil (of course we had no bags as we hadn't planned to stay overnight), I felt her eyes staring at my unadorned ring finger and looking into my heart, seeing not only our lie but our lack of respect for her culture and, worse, the true hollowness of our relationship, which was based on so little and had not had a chance to grow strong.

Once in our small, clean room, though, we were safe. We

could lock the door and relax our guard. We laughed at our having duped the old woman. As if we cared – now – that she disapproved of us. Who cared about anything? The old lady's bed was ancient, solid, sealed tight with pristinely laundered sheets. It made a perfect arena, a wrestling ring, for unthinking, careless sex. When we went out later for something to eat, there were the eyes drilling into us as we left, and as we returned, the eyes that spoke of decency trampled on, religion insulted. I was glad to leave the next morning.

Back in the city, Neil's wholesale hoovering up of everything on offer resumed. We went to all-night film shows in an amphitheatre, lying full-length on the tiered seats and dozing as dawn came up. We even went to Cinecittà to sign up as film extras, as we were running out of money and Neil had heard that anyone could get a walk-on part, provided they had some smart clothes to wear (we didn't, but we could sort that out once we got some work). When we got to the production office, early in the morning, we found a queue of desperate people already lined up, waiting for it to open: tramps and drug addicts by all appearances, and again I felt the shame that was coming to characterise this time for me. We were dropouts too.

In the end it was the pimple that finished it off.

Neil had developed a pimple in his armpit that he couldn't leave alone. He would stand in front of the mirror with his arm up over his head, squeezing and pressing at the bubo with his other hand. At first I teased him about it and told him to leave it alone, but I would come back from the loo or the kitchen and he would be having another go at it. I found it repulsive – I was as fixated on it as he was. I started to watch Neil, waiting for him to have another poke at his armpit so that I could bark at him not to. The fact that he couldn't stop touching it made him seem weak in my eyes; the pustule was undermining his entire personality. I'm surprised it didn't start talking, telling me he was dirty and vain.

Neil was shocked and hurt when I told him I had decided to go home before the end of his time in the flat. In all the whirlwind of our activity, he hadn't been aware of my increasing sense of alienation.

By the time I got back to England, it was nearly time to leave for Italy again. I don't really know why I bothered to come back – probably just to show my face at home and to reassure my parents that I had not had a huge tattoo, or a crewcut, or a baby. Letters began to arrive from Neil, still in Rome. It was disturbing that one or two of them were written on the back of blurry photocopies of nude drawings of myself done by Neil. And he had collaged other things onto the drawings: an empty packet of contraceptive pills, a scrap of newsprint. Stranger still, *the letters were written in Italian*. To me, already paranoid about my poor language skills, this seemed like deliberate taunting. And also phoney. But I think he had been there long enough to start thinking in Italian. It was as if Neil squeezed so much experience into his life that that summer in Rome was the equivalent of about three years lived at the pace of a normal existence.

For my part, I learnt that going out into the world was not enough to change a scared girl into an adventuress.

Chapter 13

ITALIAN MEATBALLS

The main problem is the people ... If you meet Italians they don't see any of the characteristics that differentiate you from other people, they just treat you like the quaint and archaic creature which is the English stereotype in Italian eyes.

Extract from letter home, 3 December 1982 (age 20)

FOR my year out I had a job as an English-language assistant at a secondary school in Siena, perhaps the most beautiful city in Tuscany. But the prospect of a year in Italy, even in that gorgeous museum-piece of a town, filled me with dread. Following my summer in Rome, I now nursed the morbid belief that every pensioner in the country was looking into my soul and seeing only the black molasses of sin. And I could still barely put a sentence together in Italian.

Finding a place to live in Siena was far from easy. By answering small ads I had found a grim room in a shut-up-looking house on one of the main roads out of town. There were absolutely no kitchen facilities, not even a fridge, and in the tiny bathroom the shower-head hung directly over the lavatory bowl. It was really primitive, but I was getting desperate. I remember writing a pathetic list of the 'positive' things about it to try to convince myself I would be all right there (number one was, 'I'll lose weight because there won't be any food'; number two was 'save time in the mornings'). The landlord demanded a cheque as the deposit, but I didn't have an Italian bank account. To the bank, where it turned out that foreigners weren't supposed to have cheque accounts. A little 'Italian business' took place: the bank clerk invited me there and then to lunch at his house so that I could meet his son and arrange to give him English conversation lessons; and, by the way, I could have a chequebook…

We walked to his house in the rain, awkwardly sharing an umbrella (which he had to hold above his head at arm's length as I was about a foot taller than him) and making extraordinarily banal conversation to fend off any sense of impropriety. I discovered that he was Signor Bartolomeo and that his son, Luigi, was a law student, currently laid up at home with a broken foot. When we arrived at their house in a back street of Siena, I was introduced to Signora Bartolomeo, who was already busy preparing their lunch. It was obvious that she was very put out by the arrival of a gangling foreigner: she had to divide up the three pieces of meat that she'd bought to make a fourth portion, and I saw from the way the knife hung uncertainly above the flesh before she cut into it that she was torn as to whether this great pale Amazon needed a larger share. I don't think I got one.

Luigi, the coddled son, a fleshy boy of about eighteen or nineteen with a slack-lipped Elvis pout, was laid up on the sofa in the gloomy *salotto*, his foot in plaster, when Signor Bartolomeo brought in the treat he had found for his darling boy: a nice plump *inglesina* for his amusement. Babbo would leave us *alone* for a little now while Mamma prepared lunch.

I sat down on a tightly stuffed armchair next to Luigi's foot and looked down at his dirty toenails. Perked up by this unexpected delivery of a girl before lunch, he hoisted himself up on his cushions and had a good look at me. I don't think he liked what he saw very much. His pout pursed itself into a critical little moue.

'So, yes, 'ello. You are at Siena long time?'

Oh no, not the dazzling display of English skills again (I was having to go through these stilted conversations with virtually everyone I met). Was this really worth it to get a chequebook? Just.

I smiled. 'No, not long – just long enough to be able to find my way around.'

He smiled too now, his eyes completely dead. He hadn't understood a word I'd said.

'So, you would like to speak English with me, yes?' This was me again – it was much easier to talk in pidgin English (although I had to be careful not to do it in my classes at the school).

'*I* would like? My *father* would like, *vairy* much!' Luigi sniggered. 'He like I *marry* English girl!' He rubbed his fingers together to indicate *moola*.

'Ri-ight, yes.'

'You want I take you dancing? I show you good time? You like *la droga*?' Now he was noisily snorting an imaginary line of coke.

Oh god. 'No, not really, thanks.'

'Is *good!* I get good stuff!'

I must have nodded by accident.

'*Sì! La coca*-eeeeeee-*na!* Make you go fast, go sexy! I get?' He hauled himself more upright on the sofa and leaned over. 'Feel this! I break my *foooot* but I not break *heeem*. He go good with *cocaina*, go for *long long* time…'

He took my hand and pulled it towards his fly.

'*Mangiamo, giovani!*' Mamma Bartolomeo came to the door in her apron, pushing the hair out of her eyes with the back of her hand. She smiled a businesslike smile. 'Ah, you make friendsheep, yes? Is good!' Clearly while I had been in the parlour with Luigi,

Signor B had been running through the advantages of the boy seeing a nice young English lady and had persuaded la Signora that it was worth the sacrifice of a sliver of *bisteca*.

We ate lunch in formal near-silence, Luigi occasionally catching my eye and then exaggeratedly rolling his gaze to the treasure down below the tabletop. Then I was able to politely take my leave. A couple of days later I got my chequebook and wrote out the deposit cheque for the rented room. Then, only hours after I had given it to the landlord, I heard about a much better room in a shared flat. I rushed back to the bank and cancelled the cheque (I didn't know the Italian for any financial transactions, but I just kept waving the chequebook and shouting *'Cancellare! Cancellare!'* It seemed to work. Just to be sure, I withdrew all the money that I had deposited earlier in the day to cover the cheque). I heard nothing more from the landlord of the kitchenless lodgings. Obviously I understand now that the 'wet room' was actually very stylish and years ahead of its time. I also never gave Luigi a single conversation lesson. Weeks later I met the bank clerk in the street and he told me sorrowfully that he was *very* disappointed in me, mostly for stopping the cheque.

On the day that I moved into my new flat, none of the four other tenants was there. In the kitchen a Siamese cat with its ribs showing through its fur was desperately trying to bite through the plastic wrapping on a bag of frozen giblets that were defrosting on the work surface. Its pitiful mewling followed me into the bedroom that I was to share with Gina, the daughter of a Glaswegian ice-cream baron. I had met her once already, when I came to view the flat; tiny and bubbly, she seemed very Italian until she opened her mouth and out came a cute, giggling Scottish voice. Two very dark Southern Italian girls shared another bedroom, sleeping head-to-toe in their single beds with their mothers or sisters if they came to visit. One of these two, Maddalena, was very aware of her good looks, fiercely made up with mud-coloured foundation and dressed to kill whenever she went into college. She kept her wardrobe fresh by going on the bus to Florence for regular shoplifting excursions. The other, Rosa, was much more thickset and defeated-looking, with heavy, black-rimmed glasses. Once we went out to the cinema together – she said she had only ever been to the movies twice before, but she told me that she wasn't afraid to be out at night with me 'because everyone will think you are a man'.

While I was unpacking my stuff and putting it into the splintered desk that also had to serve as my chest of drawers, I heard the key in the front door and then an explosion of guttural Italian. Even with my limited vocabulary, I could recognise extravagant swearing. *'Porca miseria! Oh, che cazzo di gatto! Ma, Madonna maiale! No, ma, minchia!'* I went back to the kitchen and found the cat in a pool of blood, chewing on a giblet ice-pop. Serena, sole mistress of the master bedroom, was viciously mopping up the mess and shouting at the cat in a voice which soon reduced me to the same cowering state as that poor animal (it disappeared shortly afterwards but I was too scared to ask what had happened to it).

Serena was an overbearing Northern Italian who looked down on the rest of us in the flat and considered us all to be dirty foreigners. Gina was the least reviled as she was pretty and looked like a Northerner, Maddalena and Rosa (both from the despised Deep South of Italy) came next down the pecking order, and I was bottom of the table for being so physically alien – tall, fair, awkward, with big feet. Serena nicknamed me Olive Oyl. Her voice was extraordinary, the growl of a drunken whore with a knife at your throat in a Victorian melodrama. She had the biggest room and she liked to sit in it with the door open, a spider in her web, keeping an eye on the insects. She couldn't bear it when I shut the door of our room to write letters or read and, when she could stand it no longer, would burst in without knocking and stand in the doorway staring at me suspiciously.

Serena was the only one of us with a steady boyfriend. Her Marco was more like a petit-bourgeois husband, turning up for his lunch every day in his almond-green leather trousers. Serena seemed desperate to hang on to him, perhaps to become his wifey, and she cooked his meals with great care, something I found impossible to imagine doing myself for any man. She always put a tablecloth out for him and Marco would tuck a corner of it into his shirt for a napkin. A couple of days after I had moved in, I noticed that she had started folding the tablecloth in half, so that it was only covering *their* end of the table.

There was serious trouble when Serena discovered that somebody had eaten some of Marco's meatballs, which she had prepared for him the night before, carefully noting just how many *polpette* were in the pan. When she counted them again the next day, *two* were missing, and she began to bark and curse. Of course, I was the chief suspect, but *Gina* was the meatball thief, as she told me in a hot whisper later on: 'Oh, Carrie, I just *popped* them in!'

Living in Italy just wasn't what I had expected. Bad plumbing and dodgy men aside (it's only in Italy that I have ever seen men – more than once – sitting in their parked cars masturbating…), I felt that I had somehow been brought down low. Everything seemed shoddy and second-rate. The windows of the flat rattled alarmingly every time the door to the block slammed shut. The gas canister for the cooker was frequently empty (exhausted by

Serena's marathon sessions *al forno*). Electric sockets sparked and smoked. Not only that, I was living among thieves and drug addicts. It seemed that everyone was dabbling in crime – it was so accepted that after a while you almost ceased to notice it. Maddalena would come back from one of her Florence trips and pull all the jumpers and handbags she had stolen out of carrier bags and show them off to us, pointing out a detail here, the quality of the finishing there.

Even innocent Gina, with her sad-Pierrot pyjama case and her little flowery prayer postcards blu-tacked on the wall beside her bed, fell in with some bad boys. She went away with them to a house outside Siena for the weekend and then we got a phone-call from her saying could we come and get her as she had 'gone all funny'. Two of us took a taxi and went to pick her up. On the way back, her head lolled on my shoulder and she snuggled into me in an uncomfortably trusting and cuddlesome way, as though she thought she would be *safe* with me (perhaps *she* thought I looked like a man as well). The boys, it turned out, had given her pills to take. She had had no idea what they were: 'Oh, Carrie,' she said, 'I just *popped* them in.'

Alessio was a keen anglophile and liked to have an English girlfriend. I met him very casually, as one met most people in Siena, sitting in the sun in the Piazza del Campo. He already knew some of the other English girls who I was with, had in fact been going out with one of them, but he soon transferred his affections. I think it was because I looked more obviously English than her, and when he found out I was keen on pop music, that was it. One of the first things he did was to serenade me with his guitar, in English – he was 'so crazy' about Neil Young and Peter Gabriel. He gave me some black-and-white photos of himself leaning with the guitar against a graffiti-ed wall, looking like an Italian Joe Strummer. He was *so* proud of those photos.

It was funny to have spent all these months in Italy being ridiculed for my Englishness (I had stopped being hurt by the comments about my 'English teeth', my incredible height, the size of my feet, my 'terrible' accent), only to find, now that I was suddenly on the 'inside' and hanging out with young Italians, that in fact Englishness was what they craved. Englishness was *'cool'*, although they were careful not to get carried away. They wanted to give a surface impression of Englishness – a hip T-shirt, the latest records – whilst remaining passionately grounded in their own culture. These *ragazzi* were fairly up-to-date with current trends; they were amused by *'il punk'*, although they wouldn't be seen *dead* in such scruffy clothes. I gave them my tapes of Duran Duran, Spandau Ballet and Yazoo after tiring of evenings spent with four or five Italians bending reverently over my portable cassette player. Even Alessio, with his love of English pop culture ('You know what is "Mary Jane"? Is *la droga*!! You know this song of the Beatles, called your name? On the White Album? Oh, you *don't know*!'), religiously cooked himself a little tomato sauce every evening to spoon over his pasta. I can't smell fresh sage without remembering him holding a bunch of it to my nose and telling me I didn't eat properly. English stuff was fashionable, but they all had a hot coal of Italian pride glowing inside them – for their buildings, their food and wine, their roads, their football – for everything, really, except their laws.

Alessio seemed to be immensely popular: a stroll through town involved a constant pantomime of greetings to his numerous friends. It was ages before I realised the complex hand-signals he made to all these acquaintances were covert communications about the soft drugs he peddled. He was charming, you might say manipulative: occasionally I was unwittingly co-opted to play a part in his petty crimes. Once we were wandering around the open-air market when he stopped at a stall selling sunglasses.

'Ask how much they are,' he murmured and I did, not realising until afterwards that I was being used as a distraction while Alessio pocketed a couple of pairs. (Sunglasses operated as a sort of alternative currency, as it seemed dope-peddlers were always happy to accept a pair of shades as payment for drugs.)

It was good having a boyfriend. It made life seem much more normal, and I felt less exposed to all-comers. I had slipped beneath the surface of the country and I liked it better on the inside. Alessio shared a flat very similar to ours on the other side of Siena and I used to spend a lot of time there with him and his two flatmates. They were remarkably easy-going about the accommodations that were necessary to fit me in. To begin with Alessio's room-mate made himself scarce when I was staying overnight, but later on he didn't bother to sleep elsewhere, creeping in when we were both asleep. Our barn-style proximity seemed a little shameful, but I sensed these boys were conforming to centuries-old norms, ways of getting by when rooms were shared: there was a shy acceptance that a woman was a woman and must be enjoyed while the going was good. (I wasn't unaware of the fact that, as an English girl, I was considered 'easy'. A young Italian man would think himself very savvy to find an English or German girlfriend who would willingly sleep with him, whilst the good Catholic Italian girls saved themselves for marriage – of course the good Catholic boys would be wanting to marry a virgin when the time came.)

Sleeping with Alessio was fun – and he seemed pretty excited to be sleeping with me – but the fun nearly had to stop when he became worried that his penis was falling apart. I couldn't see anything wrong with it, but for a while he had a very Italian neurosis about the little arches of skin connecting the inside and the outside – he thought they were wearing out (surely this was just so much transparent guilt about our happy appetite for each other?). I am sure he wanted to ask his mamma if his *uccellino* was all right and not about to wither away altogether.

One weekend we did go over to the coast to visit his mamma (but not to ask her about *that*) and Alessio wanted us to have sex in the lavatory on the train. I wasn't against the idea, but there just wasn't room so we ended up having a wee together instead and that seemed to make him happy enough. When we got to Pesaro, I was very warmly and sweetly scooped up by Alessio's mother and sisters and subjected to the most charming interrogation. (Alessio had disappeared into his old bedroom where his adolescence was carefully preserved, including precious boxes of Emerson, Lake and Palmer LPs which I would soon have to listen to and appear to enormously enjoy.) In the *salotto* with his family it was like an old anthropological documentary, with indigenous tribeswomen welcoming the lady explorer into their communal hut. They touched my hair… looked covertly at my giant's feet… a gift of beads was made… The beads were rose quartz – cool, pink, heavy globules. Alessio was impressed by his mother's gift and told me that the pink stones represented 'true love'. All weekend, as Alessio's family wrapped me in their hospitality, I could see the light of hope in his mother's eyes – would her boy marry this *straniera?* Would she take him away to make his fortune across the sea? All we needed was a headscarf for me and Ellis Island looming into view off the starboard bow.

****

Carrie Jones

My job as a language assistant ended in May and I made the long journey home by train. After a couple of weeks at home I hotfooted it back to Cambridge where I had discovered there was actually something called the 'summer term', a kind of secret session reserved for swots and people with no family life. Perfect.

Alessio was coming to stay with me and I went down to meet him off the train at Victoria. As he materialised out of the crowds hurrying along the platform, the three long, hot days it had taken him to reach me were clearly delineated in the three yellow ringmarks of sweat under the arms of his shirt. There was no film-scene reunion by the platform barrier; we barely kissed. Alessio was very agitated and disturbed by something that had happened on the train from Dover. A skinhead had pulled a knife on the ticket inspector and had been manhandled off the train by police. Alessio wasn't shocked by the callous violence of the youth; rather, he felt a passionate empathy with the shaven-haired underdog.

'He have no money for a ticket. No *dough*. These *pigs*, they *crush* him, they *shame* him. He is fighting for his *pride of self*! They *pigs*! I read about them in *New Musical Espress*.'

He was carrying an enormous quantity of pasta and coffee packed for him by his mother, four or five large packets of spaghetti and at least two bags of ground coffee. Clearly she was worried that he would not be able to ingest adequate quantities of carbohydrate and caffeine in a strange country. I hadn't realised what a huge deal it was for Alessio to be cut adrift from the motherland – I don't think he had been abroad before.

By the time we got back to Cambridge my sense of connection to him had quietly broken. And things only got worse once we were trapped together in the college. The geeks doing the summer term were allowed to stay in the most sought-after rooms in the college, elegant apartments in the seventeenth-century central court, but Alessio loathed the formality of the buildings, the heavy-handed symbols of the college's paternal authority – the porters, the gates, the wooden signs with their hand-scripted rules and regulations, the fact that you couldn't walk on the grass. It didn't make any difference that we were on the *inside* of the institution, that the rules were supposed to make life *sweeter* for us: he felt horribly oppressed. Within a few days he was like a caged animal. One night, he peed out of the window to show his contempt for the place. The next day he spat phlegm out of the window. When we walked around the city centre, he was blind to the attractions of the shops and colleges, unmoved by the happy summer throng of tourists and students: he started stepping off the pavement into the path of bicycles, trying to unseat the riders. The only thing that moved him was the window of a rundown delicatessen near Magdalene that was filled with dusty packets of his favourite brand of pasta – he stood in front of that window like a priest before his altar.

I hated him and he hated me. He hated me now that I was back in my real context, more fully myself than the cartoon that had passed for me in Italy. And I liked him so much less now that *he* had been ripped out of his context and stripped of the confidence and verve, the swagger that had once appealed to me. In Italy I think I had seemed unfettered and careless of other people's judgement. Now I must have appeared like a pampered rich girl, in her posh college, picnicking on the lawns like Alice in Wonderland whilst every last thing was taken care of for me (he felt the same lachrymose pity for the humble woman who came in to clean my rooms as he did for the 'tragic' skinhead).

Mercifully my rooms in college included two little bedrooms, so we were able to get away from each other, but the days still seemed interminable. Then, thank God, Alessio hit on the idea of going to see Gina, and I was soon gratefully seeing him onto a coach to Glasgow and saying *'Addio'* – goodbye for ever.

Later that summer, when he was back home, Alessio sent me a letter (I've got quite a collection of these post-break-up letters). He was pretty cheerful and sounding much more like his old self. He said he'd had a wonderful time with Gina, mainly thanks to her father's generosity with the whisky bottle. Then, as he'd tried to re-enter Italy, he said he had been immediately arrested on suspicion – who knows how well-founded? – of drug-smuggling. Apparently he had phoned a well-placed uncle who got him off with the nifty application of a *bustarella,* a bribe. Now, he said, he was working as a roadie for his idols, the Clash. Again, who knows if this was true or simply face-saving *braggadoccio*? I bet it was all true.

At least while I was living in Italy I got sufficiently under the country's skin to have a boyfriend who was an archetypal young Italian male: sparky and unscrupulous, sexy, a little bit immature, and tribally proud of being Italian.

It was the second time I had lived for a sustained period as a foreigner, but my foreignness was much more apparent in Italy and I didn't speak the language as well as I spoke French. Whilst it was disconcerting to be treated as a stereotype, there was also something to be said for it. You could disappear behind the cardboard cut-out version of yourself, even playing up to people's expectations of how you would behave. Cardboard cut-outs have very few long dark nights searching for identity and trying to understand their inner conflicts. In the end, though, I prefer to be myself, conflicts and all.

Chapter 14

EXTRA-MARITAL

When I saw my room again it was just as cold and dowdy as it ever was, except that I had forgotten in the course of my daydreams about it in Italy ... I have not yet been to any parties and, alas, cannot invite you to any elegant event where young beaux will 'queue up' to dance with you! Things like that don't happen in Cambridge! The parties are all in two-up two-down houses with communal kitchens full of mouldering bean hotpots.

From a letter to my mother, 16 October 1983 (age 21)

ALL through my year out I had dreamed of how it would be when I got back to Cambridge – but it was very different now that all the other students in my year apart from the linguists had graduated and left. And all the people I'd so admired in the year above me were long gone too. There was the new intake of baby-faced first-years to try to make friends with, and we were also treated as honorary graduates, which meant mixing with the perma-students, prematurely middle-aged PhD students with grey library-tanned skin and no sense of humour.

I felt that I had lost my sexual standing. Suddenly I was nobody. Before I had gone to Italy my self-confidence had relied on the faint aura of notoriety that I had felt surrounded me. Because it buoyed me up to feel that I was attracting attention, I was able to experience it as a sort of admiration, even if that wasn't always the case. That feeling of being different, singled out, easily transmutes itself into a feeling of superiority. In that narrow community I had been the most minor of minor celebrities, famous only for being good fun *and* a lefty (actually, maybe I should take more credit for achieving the near impossible), but the feeling that I was *watched*, just sometimes, rather than ignored, was enough to make me feel hyper-alive, shiny, electrified. Now, though, all the networks that had carried the knowledge of me as successfully flirty, a little bit outrageous, always good for a party, had been dismantled. I was back at square one. And so I reverted to the behaviour that had characterised me as a first year: a series of puppy-dog crushes on men who didn't deserve my rather desperate adulation – and who certainly didn't want it.

It was very slim pickings among the graduate students. Quite a few of them actually seemed to be mentally ill. There was a tiny bushbaby of a man from Malaysia who obsessively collected rubber bands and kept them in an ever-growing ball that he tossed from hand to hand. Another cleared his throat constantly and would spin round to check for imaginary stalkers every few minutes. Yet another would stop as he crossed the court to stare intensely at his watch, then turn around and retrace his steps. It was a Lewis Carroll world.

The graduates fell into two crude sub-groups: there were the pre-aged weirdos who had already sculpted the personas they would go on to inhabit for the rest of their tenured lives as academics, only honing their eccentricities as they crumbled into senility. Then there were the others, who still vaguely remembered being young and happy and who made wild and disastrous attempts to reconnect with their younger selves, the way they had been before academe squeezed the life out of them. These included the guy who tried to peroxide his hair and then, seeing that it now looked like a sheepskin rug, hacked at it with blunt scissors, before finally having an insanely ill-advised session with the henna powder after one too many joints. Others groped for even more junior versions of themselves and organised teddy bears' picnics or Beetle drives.

Among these Tweedledums and Tweedledees there were one or two who had escaped the academic crusher and were still recognisably human, likeable even. My diminished ego sought comfort in unrewarding crushes on these few. There was Max, a German law student, whose appeal — such as it was — lay in his nice manners and the latex look of his skin. What is it about men with sallow, rubbery-looking skin that turns me on? Those thin ridges around their mouths when they smile... it's not that attractive *per se*, but it's a look that reminds me of the first boy I ever had a serious crush on. The boy in the school orchestra, Jamie Callan, whose love for me was derailed by the falling apart of my Jesus sandals, had that same elasticity in his features, the same blue-grey tinge to his cheeks. My young addiction to him was born out of nothing more than our proximity: every morning our thighs would brush as we honked out 'Glad That I Live Am I' or some other hymn on our clarinets. But our time sharing a music stand seems to have stamped me with a liking for a very particular type of man that looks as though it will probably last all my life. Another *ur*-boy is the overgrown baby with wide eyes and sticking-up hair, yet another the crop-haired socialist intellectual. All were original objects of my unrequited love and I have been looking for replicas of them ever since.

My search for men with certain physical characteristics, usually facial, strikes me as akin to ducklings, who learn to follow whatever creature or form they first see at birth. Usually it's their mother, but it can be a human or a dog, say, or even a ball.

Carrie Jones

The intense but immature feelings I had for those early crushes must have imprinted their forms into my brain. Most of them were childhood darlings, and I find that, even as I grow older, I still find boyish men attractive, a trait which is bound to make me seem ever more foolish.

I was foolish, too, at a garden party when, very drunk on Pimm's, I tried to waltz with rubbery German Max to an imaginary orchestra. Very disapproving, with a cold fixed smile and his teeth clamped together, Max insisted he should take me home immediately. This was no ploy to take advantage of my relaxed guard. It was a curt frogmarch to my door, possibly with the well-meant intention of sparing me any further embarrassment, possibly just stopping short of a punishment beating. Once I had seen the very Teutonic way Max dealt with my 'degeneracy', I no longer found him so appealing.

My other crush victim was an affable blond called Douglas – *he* harked back to Kitten-Face, the adorable fluffy blond boy who edited the college newsletter during my first year and for whom I spent endless hours typing and stapling, all for love, all for nothing. Douglas had the same silly giggle, the same air of empty-headed sweetness; he wore shorts and a blazer all summer long and was always to be found standing at one of the endless college garden parties with a glass of warm white wine and a vacuous smile, his scalp turning crimson under his wispy blond hair.

The only sex I had the whole year was a dreadful episode with a super-arrogant medic who couldn't stop laughing at the ease with which he barked me into bed. In the course of one bitterly regretted weekend, I let him take photographs of me in the nude *and* I caught the most painful throat infection I have ever had – made worse by my conviction that the virulence of his germs was somehow linked to his being a trainee doctor. I included a long and detailed description of my symptoms in a letter home, but naturally omitted to say that they had been caused by a rogue blowjob.

In spite of the overwhelming evidence that studying for a PhD turned you boring overnight, I sleepwalked into starting one myself. When I woke up I was in a library behind a small barricade of fusty books. My face was pleated with the imprint of my sweater sleeve and a globule of dribble hung from my watch. Panicking that I would be locked in the library for ever, I ran to escape.

The decade was already half over, but *my* Eighties began on July 29th 1985. I had moved to London where I managed to get a job in publishing. It was very ill-paid, but it was the sort of work that brought me into (albeit fleeting) contact with celebrities who were having their moment under the bright lights of that overlit decade: George Michael, Julie Burchill, Tony Parsons, Paula Yates, Malcolm McClaren, Ken Russell. There always seemed to be a film preview to go to, or a record label launch: I was a very willing extra in the promo crowd. I lived on canapés. Whenever I went back North to visit home, it was obvious that no one believed the tales I told about my new London life. Did they think I had a Billy Liar complex?

It took me so little time to reinvent myself. My transformation from earnest student activist to (as I saw it) media babe around town was achieved with such speed that I was like a TV makeover, all surface glam barely hiding wonky staples and splintered, unpainted insides. I did everything at a run; I always had invitations on my mantelpiece, but most of my new friends were actually someone else's. I knew what was smart, I could drop names with the best of them, but I wasn't getting very far under the skin of this new society. At the same time I was turning up my nose at the way of life I'd had before. I no longer loved the fug of communal kitchens, the comfy chaos of student life. It's funny to look back and see that my life has mirrored, not to say parodied, the times in which I lived. Except that, although I may have hung out in the Groucho Club and at the Criterion Brasserie, although I may have had Morrissey's phone number and met Vivienne Westwood, I didn't really have a place in that world. Underneath I always felt like a fraud.

It was such a conformist decade, and I was comforming my heart out, making sure that everything was done according to the manual and that my puffball skirt and mirror shades were just so. (I've got hilarious photos of myself posing for an imaginary pop video down at Docklands when it was first being developed – I'm staring 'seductively' through wire mesh, shades on and hair gelled vertical.) The men I was involved with during this time were wonderfully Eighties too. I met them all through work and they were like badges of office, or Brownie badges, sewn onto the giant shoulder-pads of my power-suit jacket. *Have you got your TV Presenter yet?* No, but I'd got my Film Producer, Gossip Columnist and Hot New Writer, my Record Sleeve Designer and my Record Company Boss…

All these men came my way purely because of my job, and I believe that was the main reason why I was attractive to them – at least initially. Work was everything then. The entire structure of my life was predicated on it, my social life dictated by it. The idea was that your work was fun, but you were in no doubt that fun was work too. Never forget it. Contacts, networking, keeping up with trends – every second counted. I was so caught up in the spin that when someone came my way on a completely different trajectory I was quick to push him away again. Too quick…

I'm looking at a Christmas card sent to me a decade ago. It features a photo of the sender's little children draped in tinsel. I feel strange looking at their faces with their slightly stiff coached smiles. Inside the card are the words *'I will always love you'* – but it was the conception of the youngest of the children, twins, which ended my relationship with their father. More or less.

The person who sent me the card was John Elland. In looks he was different from everyone else I have ever been involved with – dark and very masculine, with strong, well-defined features and crisp, wiry hair. His appearance didn't link back to any early passion of mine; no teenage proto-Johns were hanging around in my memory. This made it hard for me to see how attractive he was, and for a while I was more or less blind to his sexy muscularity. We were at college together, but I don't really have any clear memories of him from that time. We didn't go out with each other until I had moved to London. I don't even remember *that* time with very much clarity, apart from the bus journey to his house in Finsbury Park, which went past Holloway Prison – the massive, drab flanks of the place never failed to make me fearful that some terrible circumstance might one day see me locked up there.

The fragility of my new persona meant that my relationship with John didn't stand much of a chance. He had let out all the spare bedrooms in his big Victorian house to friends. The group of them seemed very tightly bound up with each other and to somehow promote the values they shared as a group in a way that fatally exposed the shallowness of *my* new, shiny lifestyle. They were clever and cynical, and would certainly never let it look as though they were trying. They might end up doing the sorts of jobs that got you a partnership and share options after a few years but for now they were urban bohos, staying up late talking and drinking, laidback, articulate observers of a world they didn't yet want to join. They weren't impressed by me, and I could feel the gloss rubbing off my newly acquired glamour before it had even had a chance to dry. Whenever I was in that big, shadowy house in Finsbury Park, I felt like a child who wasn't allowed to touch anything or join in the grown-ups' conversation. Besides, you could *never* get into the bathroom in the morning.

Acting alone, I could convince myself I had undergone a Cinderella transformation, but sharing my life with someone else forced me to see the reality that still lay beneath, the reality of an ordinary little person. John had an enormous bed, but all I could see was the greyness of the sheets. I don't remember actually finishing with him, but his name vanishes from my 1986 diary after a few weeks.

A few years later, John got back in touch with me and we arranged to meet up for a drink after work. It turned out that he was now married with a young child. This didn't have the impact on me that it perhaps should have done, being still so far outside my own glimpsed possibilities that I was scarcely able to imagine one of my friends' lives having been transformed in this way. Besides, marriage had never been a lovely thing to me. All my direct experience of it – my parents' and grandparents' marriages – had been of ill-disguised contempt, coldness, miserable attempts to patch up the dreary status quo, and discreet temporary escapes. It was even whispered that my grandmother had been blackmailed into marrying her second husband because of what he knew about her tax returns. You couldn't tell me that marriage was warm and cosy, a flannel-lined fortress against the world which must on no account be violated. So I didn't treat

John's new status as husband and father with much awe. Anyway, that was his business. He wasn't saying much about it.

Neither was I. In spite of my low opinion of marriage, I was engaged to a boy called Ed. He had asked me and I had said yes because, when the moment came, it was lovely to say yes, it made both of us feel wonderful. It would have been so churlish to deny this moment of happiness – and accepting a proposal seemed entirely unconnected to the idea of *being married* and of *having children*. I never thought about this prospect with any realism. By the time John got in touch, I knew for certain that I wasn't going to marry Ed. I had lost all interest in sex with him, and for a long time my body had felt completely deadened. It was a cause of sadness and worry, because I wanted desperately to be able to sustain a relationship beyond the first year or so of novelty and lust.

It still makes me sad to think that Ed and I spent years together and that I dismissed him from my life with absolute certainty – the act of dismissal undermined all the time that we had had together, bringing my judgement (and his) into question. If he was so wrong for me, why did it take years, and a failed engagement, to find out?

The night John and I met up again, in June, it was overwhelmingly hot and, after our drink, we went into Hyde Park and walked by the Serpentine in the darkness. I had never been in the park at night and it felt very threatening at first. Surely anyone going there at this time must be up to no good, like us. Men, alone or in twos, walked past us, glancing at us to see if we too were on the prowl, or to see if we posed a threat. I saw what I thought was envy in the eyes of one or two, that our pairing was already negotiated.

The water was gorgeously still, with the lights of the hotels on

Park Lane licking at its surface. One or two cars passed silently by. The air was moist and hot and it created an exhilarating illusion of incorporeality: as my body temperature matched the temperature of the air around it, I felt that I was evaporating into the atmosphere, losing all sense of boundary between myself and the world. John and I sat down on a bench and watched the twinkly water in silence, immersed in the dissolved light and air. The moment was heading inevitably towards a kiss and it was simply a question of waiting, just a moment or two longer, enjoying the knowledge that it was going to happen. I turned my cheek to touch his and felt his skin damp with the heat. A little turn more and our mouths touched. It was a ravishing kiss.

Those parts of me that had become dead to sensation during the years with Ed burst into spangly, sequinned responsiveness. Gone was the awkwardness, the horrible self-awareness that had dogged my increasingly joyless efforts to be intimate with Ed whilst wanting to run away and hide. Everything about this sultry night in the park was thrilling: the solid flesh of John's arms beneath his hot, clean-smelling cotton shirt, the change from smooth skin to bristled skin as I kissed his face, the slick of sweat in the hair at the back of his neck, even the stern cloth of his work suit felt pleasurable. It was very late now and something from real life intruded and made me think I should go home. So I stood up on shaky legs and we kissed again, pressing hard into the full length of each other's bodies. Things were set inexorably in motion that beautiful Whistlerian night and I knew that I would see John again, in spite of his marriage. I didn't feel so bad about betraying my own relationship. I felt I was sloughing the dead skin off it.

Over that summer John and I often took risks in order to be together. It was wonderfully lustful and, although I felt guilty, it was guilt at one remove – guilt which is not actually *felt* but only acknowledged as the correct emotion to feel. I never thought about his marriage and what state it must be in for him to be sleeping with me; I just thought, *he wants me*, and didn't question why. The truth is I enjoyed the wrongness of what we were doing and I got off on the risks we took. There was a slight air of farce about the whole business: we did all the clichéd things people do when they're having an illicit affair. The need to keep everything secret took me right back to the secrets I kept as a child, and through the secrecy I got in touch with my true sexual self (so carefully hidden).

One early evening, in a quiet corner of Green Park, John and I were just another couple lying together in the long grass, kissing, kissing, kissing. Then, I don't know how discreetly – perhaps not discreetly at all – we shifted and slipped and unzipped and made love. It's no good, I *can't* say 'made love'; it's a horrible phrase and I hate it. We had sex. As John moved inside me, I saw the punched brown-leather brogues and tweedy turn-ups of a gentleman passer-by. I saw his feet hesitate, receive the shock of what he was seeing. I closed my eyes to hide from him and when I peeped again he had gone. I didn't care. I did feel a spritz of embarrassment but it wasn't enough to extinguish the powerful heat of doing it anyway.

It was the not caring which felt so good. Once I had smiled the smirk of transgression, that Princess Di classic with the upturned eyes and the coded lips, I was lost. I went over to the side of exultant pleasure and it seemed self-justifying. When John's wife went away for the weekend with their little girl, I arrived to take her place. He was still living in the same house where I had felt so pathetically shy when I was his girlfriend the first time round. Now that he was married, all his friends had moved out, and the house was filled with his wife's belongings. It was hard not to think that it might have been *my* things strewn about the rooms, if I had had a better sense of myself, more confidence, when I had first been involved with him. I had been so stupid.

What seemed to justify everything was to have returned from the sexual dead. It really was a resurrection, a miracle. To feel again, nerve endings reactivated; to stand at a different tilt, see a different outline in the mirror. What happened to me when I was fucking John was amazing. One moment I was avoiding sex with Ed by any strategy I could devise and feeling *ugly* (which of those feelings comes first? They feed each other). Then, wonder of wonders, I find myself in bed with John and the strangest things begin to happen. Legs growing longer, lither…arms silky, trim…stomach, *what* stomach?…hair lashing about like galloping ponies (my neat bob, that is)…breasts pert and peachy. But above all, there is the transformation of the bottom, that greyish appendage I normally wish to tear from my bones with my bare hands. It's changing! Hitherto undiscovered muscles are reeling it in, remoulding it, honing it down, tuning it up… The effect wasn't permanent. It wore off between applications; but as a means of improving my self-image, sex with John was unbeatable.

It wasn't all about sex. In my diary for 1990, one Sunday just says 'day out'. This is code for a strange day when John and I went to Henley-on-Thames for the day, and his little girl – let's call her Anna – came too.

Anna was asleep in the car when John came to pick me up. I got into the front passenger seat and turned round to look at her. Her eyes opened and she stared at me silently. She was silent all the way to Henley.

I wasn't sure we ought to be doing this. We walked along the High Street towards the river. We must have looked like a perfect little family. I was carrying the bag of nappy-change equipment, but I was keeping myself separate from John and his baby. I didn't want to challenge Anna for his attention and I had no idea what effect my appearance in her mother's usual place might be having on her.

Here was the Thames, as sunny and genial as a head boy on prize-giving day. We hired a small motorised boat, a Meccano toy for grown-ups, called *Waterbaby*. The name was not auspicious. Anna didn't like sitting between us on the seat while John steered the boat. She began to cry, and then to say 'Mummy' with chillingly pure diction, like a beautiful and very expensive doll.

I don't know whether John had a *reason* for organising the day out. I doubt it. He wasn't into reasons. It wouldn't have been to see how I got on with Anna. And he would never have thought of using Anna as cover so that he and I could spend time together. I'm sure he simply thought it would be a nice thing to do. He didn't have much time for the awkwardnesses that arise when convention is flouted.

We chugged up the sparkling river, past the wooden summer houses with their treasured waterside lawns and frisky dogs. Our metal tub rocked in the wakes of plastic pleasure boats pushing past while Anna became more and more unhappy. Her cheeks were streaked with wind-dried tears. Then John let her steer the boat and she cheered up. But the wind grew colder and Anna needed to put her cardigan on, forcing her to relinquish control of her big new toy to me. Furious, she set about prising each of my fingers from the wheel while John tried to bend her arms into the cardigan.

I was so unused to children then. I hardly ever came into contact with them, I knew very little about the intensity of their moods and pleasures. It was almost impossible for me not to interpret Anna's wails as resentment of my presence, despair at the absence of her mother. John was being such a wonderful daddy, unstinting in the attention he beamed onto his little girl; I thought the best thing I could do was to withdraw as much as possible, try to be invisible, and let them have a nice time together.

When we came in to the riverbank to collect conkers, Anna began to show a more charming side, hopping around, fetching things, climbing over John like a squirrel. I found it very moving to see them happy together. I lay down in the grass and closed my eyes, relaxing for the first time. Suddenly John leant down and kissed me, taking me by surprise. When I looked up, I saw Anna standing over me, sternly bug-eyed, mouth pursed. We all played together then, and in the end Anna granted John's request to give me a peck on the cheek. By the end of the day I had rather fallen for her – I thought she was clever and funny, a darling. I didn't want to have made her confused or unhappy.

I thought a lot about Anna and the part she might possibly play in my future. I moved out of the flat I had shared with Ed and I allowed myself to consider all sorts of futures that included John. He said he loved me. He said it over and over again. I tried to get a clear view of what was happening but it was impossible. Was it just a sordid extra-marital affair? Was he simply incapable of being faithful? Or was I somehow special so that this was different? I wrote down long lists of questions that I wanted to ask John – chains of 'if's and 'would you?'s and 'then what?'s, which I never actually asked him. I felt that there should be some sort of resolution to the situation, and it did seem to be coming, somehow. John had never cared for conventionality. He told his wife about us and he even suggested that we all live together – I don't know how she reacted, *God knows*, but suddenly the resolution I longed for did come. Well, a resolution came, but not one I had ever imagined. One night John came to see me at my new place and told me that his wife was pregnant again.

As it happened, so was I.

I had recently got caught up in a strange medical looking-glass world. I had been for a gynaecological check-up and, whilst at the hospital, been asked if I would take part in some research on the relationship between weight and fertility. I had agreed, and, after some experiments in which I was made to wear a fishbowl helmet which analysed my breath whilst I did exercises, I was told that I had low fertility and would probably need to take the drug Clomid if I wanted to conceive. Not having any plans to have a baby at that time, I was rather blasé about this news and considered it nothing more than a licence not to worry unduly about contraception. But it had turned out to be inaccurate. I was perfectly able to conceive and it was a disaster.

John and I agreed on an abortion and I arranged it and underwent it. It was done under anaesthetic at a private hospital. I was able to bear the procedure, the shame, the misery shared with too many other girls in that place, by tuning out and switching off my mind. In the room where the anaesthetic was administered, a radio was playing pop music, presumably to help put the patients at their ease. As I sank into the hallucinogenic state of painlessness, the radio, chillingly, played 'It Must Be Love' by Madness. The horrible inappropriateness of that sweet, blithe song was amplified and distorted into something even worse by my drugged mind. If I hear the song now, the things I felt are still encoded in it.

John and I stopped seeing each other. We had had a very painful lesson, and he went back to his marriage and that other pregnancy. I was terribly sad. Even now, writing this, I'm crying, though my own kids are just here, dancing to pop music with their friends.

It was about two years later when John sent me that card. The photo showed Anna and the twin babies that John's wife had been expecting. I felt a mixture of curiosity and perturbation when I saw the hitherto abstract reason for the end of my relationship with him transformed into two chuckling toddlers: sending it did seem somewhat thoughtless in the circumstances. And what was the point of his saying he would 'always love me', since he also said it would be better if we continued not to see each other? To be loved, that's rare, and precious, but the pain of being denied that love is equal and opposite.

A motorbike drew up outside my place. A tall figure was coming to the door, ringing the doorbell. Through the glass I could see whoever it was taking off his crash-helmet.

It was him, *John*.

For whatever motive (nostalgia, backtracking, disaffection with the present) I had got in touch with John again, after years and years. I'd called him and now he had come. He was *huge* in his bike leathers. I'd never dreamt he would come on a motorbike. It seemed to change his nature entirely. Everything I'd known about him was replaced by this image of a man in leathers. And yet he was smiling, taking off his jacket. An amazing smell of warmth, leather and clean sweat spoke to me before he did.

He stood and looked at me. I kissed that smell. I kissed his cold-hot mouth, the lips chilled, the tongue warm. I kissed the cool planes of his cheeks, his burning neck. I took him to my bedroom and he fucked me. It was my idea of perfect sex. Sex with all the overtones and subtexts, the agonising, taken out. Just sex. But with someone you love and who you hope loves you. I did still love him.

Afterwards I turned and put my arm around John.

"Hello."

"Er, hi."

"That was… well. Long time no see."

"Nice way to greet me."

I shocked myself that day, having sex with a man I hadn't seen for years without even stopping to say hello first.

That was the first time of the third time that I was involved with John. His life had become still more complicated. So much time had passed since the end of our last affair and now he was divorced, remarried, with more children. I'm not sure what it was that sustained my skeletal relationship with John. Why did he bother when his life was already teeming with women? It was more than mere availability, and it wasn't out of pity – some connection definitely still existed between us, but it was so stretched as to have lost all its elasticity, it could no longer pull us together. The after-echo of a past relationship, its tense was 'might have been'. He wasn't *hungry* for me, he didn't need me. But by that stage I was grateful that he came at all.

Since then, I've hardly seen John at all. The brief sequence of afternoons that constituted the 'third time' petered out because of his work and his travelling and his commitments to other women. There was no falling out, just a lack of momentum and a mismatch in the degree of neediness we had – him, none; me, too much. If I see him, I will still want to be with him, to dig with my bare hands through the layers and layers of women with prior claims to him, trying to reach him, but it will be impossible. He is lost to me in the fractals of an extraordinarily complex and turbulent life, constantly travelling, constantly searching for the kind of adventures that demand the money and nerve of someone surfing an entrepreneurial wave. Sometimes I fantasise that he offers me the chance to work on some project with him and I throw in my job and head off to New York or Buenos Aires or wherever the venture is based. We make a killing (in which I am somehow instrumental) and he realises, at last, that we make the perfect partnership. But this is laughable, even as a fantasy; I'm a tiny speck on the ground as his plane takes off for another continent.

Chapter 15

MAGIC JOURNEY

How to break out of your mould and do something completely new and exciting. You'll be amazed at how you can come to like something you at first hated.

How to conquer boredom, listlessness, lack of self-esteem, lack of heart.

Model yourself on lifestyles you admire. If you can't go the whole way, bring a little something of your dream lifestyle into being.

Changing yourself – Finding yourself – Being yourself. Do something you've always wanted to do but never dreamed you would.

Notes for a book on 'Self-Expression' (never written), 1992 (age 30)

AS I entered my thirties it was becoming obvious that my sex life had a recurring and depressing pattern: intense excitement and desire to begin with, followed (if the relationship survived long enough) by a slow winding-down into indifference and finally a sad, rather childish repulsion. Sooner or later I seemed to find all my men wanting. Only my secret affair with John had bucked the trend, but that was doomed by its very nature.

Part of the problem with my relationships (those that developed beyond mere groping) is that I have never been *choosy* enough, always simply grateful that someone wanted *me*. But, having grabbed what was offered, in each successive relationship the blameless man's perceived physical imperfections or tics have loomed larger and larger until they obscure any balanced picture of the real person: this man smelt metallic, this one ate with his mouth open, this one left the steering-wheel of the car sticky, this one blew his nose too much, this one mumbled… I always ended up rejecting my lovers, never settling down into sustained and comfortable intimacy with them, even though that was the very thing I *thought* I wanted. With hindsight, it seems that I was deluding myself with my dream of 'true intimacy'; I can see that I have found it difficult to *handle* the physical reality of men. Literally and figuratively. The truth is that I have enjoyed less *hands-on* relationships rather more: all those lovely crushes and all the boys who lived so far away but wrote such *sweet* letters. They were easier to love and so much less demanding.

It was always tempting to search for reasons why my relationships failed in the physical make-up of my boyfriends. One had a very small penis and it was easy to blame that nub of flesh for my dissatisfaction (even though it is Agony Aunt Mantra No. I that *size doesn't matter*). But when a later boyfriend revealed an enormous one (the only word that seemed adequate for it was *schlong*), it too turned out to have its downside, namely the near impossibility of making it ejaculate (he was the one with the sticky palms and it has just occurred to me that perhaps the two things were related). I have always tended to fetishise the penis, have always been vulnerable to the belief that there's a *perfect* one that could make everything happen according to your fantasies. Yet once I start looking at pictures of them (and these days there's no need to buy third-rate magazines to get a coy glimpse of flaccid flesh), I almost immediately begin to find them unsatisfactory – this one is too thin, this one too misshapen, this one too bent, this one too florid. It's just no good going in search of the platonic ideal of the prick. Certainly, you need to desire a man's penis, but ideally you want it to be *attached* to a desirable man, not somehow split off from him and reduced, in your mind, to the role of a dildo.

Another reason for the failure of my relationships lay in my own responsiveness, or lack of it. I never had any expectation of orgasm as a corollary to sex (even with John). I only really enjoyed sex while the initial period of excitement lasted. I often craved it, but it was always about being penetrated and about the knowledge that I was desired. I 'got off' on being desired but I was conscious, from start to finish, of wanting to ensure the man was satisfied and, even more importantly, pleased with me for making it so. During sex it was as if my 'self', the kernel of thoughts and senses that constitutes my 'being-a-person', was flying apart, losing all coherence. All I was aware of was a flailing, panicking, desperate desire to 'respond properly', a horrible mire of second-guessing and failing confidence. 'Responding properly' meant, in essence, acting. I wanted to 'do it right'; but in trying so hard I ensured that I did it wrong, because I actually *felt* nothing. In failing to concentrate on my own sensations, the circuits that would have led me to an orgasm were disabled, unplugged. I had *never* had an orgasm, although I faked them pretty well.

In fact I had never really thought about orgasms or the absence of them in my life. I really hadn't. Not like my friend Susanne at college, who announced one lunchtime that she and her hairy Canadian boyfriend were going to spend the afternoon having sex until she had an orgasm. They had made their minds up and that was that. The Canadian bear had a selflessly determined set to his shoulders. I did not like to think of the role that his bearded lips might play in the exercise. Later, much later, they reappeared, triumphant. Susanne had had not one mere orgasm, but *thirty-six* — they had both counted them. *Really*.

A book was published telling women how to have an orgasm.

Of course I was too shy to buy it, but I read large sections of it in the Trafalgar Square branch of Waterstone's (lurking in a corner next to the men furtively flipping through books by 'Anonymous'), committed the salient points to memory, and made up my mind that I too would have them. Perhaps not thirty-six, but just one or two would be nice for a start.

The launch of my orgasm campaign coincided, perhaps not entirely by chance, with a holiday with my mum. For very many years we had been going away on holiday together, with me providing the companionship that my father withheld. I had always enjoyed it. I had been happy to smile benevolently when Greek waiters said, *no*, surely we *must* be sisters. I had been a little husband, an amiable escort who made very few demands. But I was starting to feel that these holidays were perhaps not quite the thing, that there might be better ways to explore the world than a watercolour holiday in Wales in the company of three bearded old ladies all called Margaret, or Christmas in a summer holiday flat in Cornwall with damp foam mattresses and not enough fifty-pence pieces for the voracious electricity meter. If I fathomed the secret of the orgasm and entered that privileged arena of the *moved*, the O-zone, I would be making some fundamental and perhaps necessary break away from her. Cracking the secret of orgasms now would be akin to stealing her toyboy – if she had one – a cruel but healthy thing to do.

When the boyfriend with the sticky palms and the alarmingly large cock began to get too much for me, I became engrossed in planning the *Magic Journey*. This was my unnecessarily twee private name for a trip around the United Kingdom in which I would take in all the places which had ever aroused my curiosity – places I had read about in biographies, places associated with artists or writers, philanthropists' model villages, the mysterious locations of standing stones or white horses, places with funny names such as Splatt and Wetwang. Like the Day of the Dead in Crouch End, it was displacement activity on a grand scale, and the Magic Journey soon started to look suspiciously like a school project. There was a folder, an itinerary, a gazetteer. I worked out the distances between destinations and anticipated where we would need to stop for the night. Brochures were sent for. By the end, I was cutting out pictures, drawing little maps, *gluing*, for God's sake.

Mum and I met up in Gloucester and drove through the Forest of Dean (made magical in my imagination by Dennis Potter's television plays), then up the Wye Valley via Tintern Abbey (mistily romanticised by Turner and Wordsworth). It was strange to be actually following the route I'd mapped out on my kitchen table in Crouch End. What had existed in my mind as perfect country roads, linking beautiful and fascinating places, were already turning out to be the usual indifferent tarmac, and the special places on my mental map were being translated into mere tourist haunts. The Forest of Dean was elusive, with barely a tree in sight as we drove past what I had imagined would be shadowy canopies of massive sycamores and oaks. Tintern Abbey was handsome, but not *Romantic*, and there was a tawdry shop selling jam and tea towels to the tourists.

From there we drove up into the Black Mountains (Bruce Chatwin had added an overlay to these for me) and found the narrow road leading to Capel-y-ffin. This was where Eric Gill, the sculptor and illustrator whose work fascinated me, had tried to establish a commune in the early part of the twentieth century. My father had a small reproduction of a Gill etching depicting a curvaceous black Eve with the serpent coiling up between her legs. He hung it low down on the wall near his record player, almost at floor level, as he always sat on the floor when he was listening to music. The potent sexuality of the image had disturbed me as a child, and I didn't approve of my father's having it to look at, in such an obviously significant, almost secret place. Then, years later, I read Fiona MacCarthy's great biography of Gill and found out that he had been highly sexualised, obsessed with sexual control and ritual, and had had an incestuous relationship with his daughter. In spite of this, I loved his work. His famous typeface, Gill Sans, designed for the London Underground, is the most perfect lettering and the font that I use for everything I write on my PC.

I had hoped that we would be able to see the place where Gill and David Jones and others had worked together, but it was hidden away somewhere and I felt too inhibited to explore private roads. The landscape was totally closed. Beautiful, but closed and quite threatening.

We gave up and drove on to Hay on Wye, to the B & B that I had booked for the night. Soon we were laying out our nighties on the pillows of twin beds just that critical twelve inches apart. Under cover of darkness and a floral polycotton duvet, those twelve inches liberated me to pursue my goal. Now that I had decided I would have an orgasm, the idea of it hovered continuously at the front of my brain. I had no real idea of what would be involved or what I was going to get as my prize, but whatever it took I was going to do it. As soon as possible.

Yet could the circumstances for my very first orgasm have been any less auspicious? The sallow goddess Anorgasmia, patron saint of chastity belts and clitoridectomies, was out to tie my hands behind my back and zap any subversive thoughts of pleasure out of my brain. Every stimulus that might have spurred me on (a man, a fantasy, a vibrator…) was absent. So many impediments (the prim pastel décor, the inhibiting quiet, the presence of my *mother*) were gathered against me. I didn't yet know enough about the nature of the beast to understand that I was reducing it to the scratching of an itch, the approach least likely to yield the swoony results I longed for. But I was nothing if not determined.

We read our novels for a little while, then it's lights out. I listen to my mother's breathing until I hear that little catch in her throat and know she's asleep. Gingerly my fingers probe between my legs. I'm not a complete stranger to my own body – no one could attend as many women's group meetings as I have and not have familiarised themselves with their sexual layout, the first commandment of feminism. But, hitherto, my explorations have only resulted in a kind of irritation, a small, mealy-mouthed discomfort that has seemed to push me away with a graceless shrug – *don't bother trying, just leave me alone.* This is what I am determined to overcome. There *must* be access to pleasure there somewhere, a locked door to the old perfumed garden. I run through the pointers from the orgasm book, so carefully memorised. Relaxation is the key. I *must* relax, must must must. The instruction to my body is completely self-defeating. Every time I check to see if I am relaxed, I find my jaw tightly clenched and every muscle taut. Ungritting my teeth and de-flexing my muscles is a weirdly active process, quite exhausting. I have a picture of myself unfolding, of smoothing out the creases of tension in my body like a linen tablecloth.

Come on then, where is it? So far I have felt nothing that could be described as pleasurable. I try to imagine a direct line between my brain and my body, a surveillance device which will pick up on the first signals of pleasure. Minutely adjusting my fingers moment by moment, I'm like a physiotherapist palpating damaged tissue. There. *There!* A tiny jot of feeling, a distant fragment of Morse code on a wrecked wire. Instantly my body goes rigid in overexcited anticipation and the jotlet vanishes. Patiently I unknot my limbs and search again for the feeble call-sign. I'm an eavesdropper at Bletchley, a smart girl soldier listening through the night for the titbit of code that will win the war. But the weather is terrible and the transmission becomes inaudible.

After the long, long day, a day during which my imagined pleasure has been bluntly translated into matter-of-fact reality – my Magic Journey turned to base metal – I'm just too tired to pursue this other imaginary goal any longer. As a formal end to my shift, I flip over onto my stomach and fall asleep.

Two days in Hay-on-Wye, two nights of frustrated friction. Two dreamy days with our heads permanently tipped to the right as we scan the spines of countless thousands of second-hand books, the sharp, damp smell of deteriorating paper constantly in our nostrils. I have the oddest sense of celebrating the luck of living in a country where the freedom and the money exist to publish such a mass, such an Everest of useless, marginal, cranky, repetitive, unreadable books. It's fantastic. I buy tattered *noirs* and romances with lurid Fifties covers, children's picture dictionaries with innocently subversive illustrations and Reader's Union editions of Arnold Bennett novels.

By night, after fish and chips or cheap Italian, my body struggles to break down the evening's delivery of grease while I grapple with my poor circuitry. Nerve endings? I seem to have dead matches instead. Nothing lights my fire. Patiently, doggedly, I try to find the magic dot of feeling again. Sometimes sensation pops up like a meerkat, only to bob down again in a nervous dash for cover.

In the orgasm manual I'd been particularly taken with a chapter that described a 'scientific study' of female masturbation. In a laboratory, discreetly blanketed women had been wired up to electrodes and then invited to bring themselves off, all the while providing a commentary on what was happening to them. Apart from the prurient appeal this had for me as a fantasy, I was intrigued by the fact that several of the women described seeing bright yellow-green light behind their closed eyes when they became aroused – brilliant expanding patches of lurid light. Now I keep looking for this light myself. As a child I was obsessed with the colours and patterns you could see with your eyes closed and used to press my eyeballs until they really hurt, just to get the kaleidoscopic effect. I try to see colour in the darkness behind my eyelids – is there really anything to see? – a flare of purple which changes to red then disappears. Everything inside me is elusive.

Something *is* happening. I'm mapping my body, triangulating my sex with a precise geometry of fingers that is gradually becoming a reliable sequence. It hasn't yet come to any kind of climax, but the same tiny steps of feeling are recognisably repeating themselves in a microscopic Riverdance. Every so often, my mind manages to lock on to the feeling and to hold it, to keep it glowing, even to enhance it for a little while before the ember loses its heat again. I can feel the warmth travelling down my muscles. And is that a lime-yellow dazzle in my mind's eye? It could be, if only I could see it properly. But it's so so tiring. My hand is cramping into a claw, and my arm – my arm aches so much. Where's the fun, the screaming ecstasy, the fireworks? The burning in my arm is out of all proportion to the intermittent promises of pleasure I'm getting and I give up. Again.

Over the next couple of days the ache intensified and my arm became all but useless – which was awkward as we were on a driving holiday and I was the driver. Using Mum's headscarf, I tried to rig up a sling to take the weight off my arm. Oddly, the worst thing was cleaning my teeth. Mum was sympathetic, though puzzled as to how the problem had flared up so severely out of nowhere. It felt like a neat rectangular block of pain, just above my elbow. In the end I had to go and see a doctor in Ludlow, where we were now staying. How wide were my eyes as I claimed total innocence of any possible cause of the acute tendonitis he diagnosed.

I was paying a high price for my ticket to fleshly heaven. But the powerful drugs I was prescribed soon knocked the pain back enough for my efforts to locate nirvana to resume. I was getting a tad despondent, even though I knew that was no sort of attitude to have: I must propagate sunny openmindedness, relaxed, carefree abandonment – essential precursors to a killer climax. In an effort to take the pressure off myself, I switched the nerve centre of the operation to our en suite bathroom. I don't know whether my mother wondered why I was spending such an incredibly long time in the bath, morning and night. Could she hear the rhythmic lapping of the water against the side of the bath? That sound really annoyed me, actually; it seemed to amplify itself inside my head until I lost all sense of connection with my poor, abraded body. And immersion *in* water didn't seem to help sensation either. But, at last, *at last*, sitting on the bathmat, I found the right combination of skin on skin. I kept it, I grew it, and, *at last*, tipped it over the edge into an orgasm. What a strange, almost painful, rush of *too-much*-ness. In fact the bit that had gone before had been much much nicer – a feeling of being suspended in warmth, of tingling laughter embedded in my flesh. The actual thing itself was almost as though my body was saying, 'Right, that's it, can't take any more of that'. It was like filling a bottle: the level rose slowly up the wide portion of the bottle, then, where the neck grew narrow, quickly raced up the rest of the way and spilled over in no time at all.

When it happened, I did smile, a tired, almost mocking smile. I was pleased I'd done it, *very* happy, but the effort it had taken was monumental. I suppose, having never really tried to do it before, not even as a child, I had had to undergo the journey from flesh-innocence to flesh-knowingness in just a few days, where other women had been on that road almost all their lives. (The closest I'd come until then was a heavenly ride on the waltzers at the fair when I was a teenager, packed into one of the round metal cars with Caroline G and two boys I really liked.)

So, yeah, I'd done it. It was a bit like when I went on the Pill for the first time. I felt I'd joined another tribe, jumped over another fence. This small, weary spasm entitled me to look the world in the eye, when *those* conversations were taking place, and to nod sagely, implying: 'Oh yes, I've had them alright'. Well, it wasn't 'them' just yet, but it soon would be. I wasn't about to stop after just one go! There was a whole lot of technique to work on, a whole lot.

But for now, that was it. The Magic Journey was over.

A few months before this adventure, I had decided that I should seek some help to tackle the recurring pattern in my relationships. I had fixed myself up with a counsellor, Christine. She was very helpful and thoughtful about all the things I wanted to discuss, but it took me a while to believe that she could really handle the tangled mess that sex had caused in my head. Christine's husband was a vicar, and to begin with I found the weekly walk up the stairs to her spare-bedroom consulting room very difficult as we had to pass all sorts of ornaments and icons, Marys and Jesuses that spoke of gentle Christian goodness and pastel conformism, qualities which would surely be insulted by my rather bleak experiences of 'family values' and 'love'. But she assured me that she could 'take it'.

I started keeping a dream diary and reading my 'best' dreams out to Christine. It wasn't really full-blown psychotherapy, but I had always been keen on Freud and it was just too tempting for me not to try to give my fifty minutes in Christine's tweedy armchair a hint of the great man's couch. I would offer my own interpretations of the week's dreams. I think it's usually a terrible indulgence to share one's dreams but, re-reading the notebook where I wrote them down, one strikes me as amusingly clunky in its symbolism. At the time I was still living with the boy with the large, reticent dick…

'I dreamt I woke up and there were bits of ash, charred paper and sparks flying through the air. Something was burning on my bedside table. It might have been this notebook, it might have been a roll of Sellotape, it might have been something edible. I had the idea that I was responsible for it spontaneously combusting and I was very afraid. I screamed and screamed for _____ to come. He seemed to take a long time to come and to be rather nonplussed. Evidently he didn't think the house was about to burst into flames. I carried on looking at the thing I had set on fire. Charred layers were peeling off and it was glowing fiercely orange underneath. There were charred dishes of food on the table and I wrote a message for _____ in the baked surface of one dish.'

This is surely an orgasm anxiety dream. So the boyfriend takes a long time to come – very literal. But he doesn't think the house is about to catch fire: he doesn't believe *I* will ever come. Yet the symbols that stand for me, for my sexuality – the dream diary, the O-shaped ring, the thing you can eat – they are already burning, glowing, and I have caused the fire, just by thinking about it… I wonder what the message was that I wrote? *I am coming so you'd better get out of the way.* When I dreamed this dream, I had already decided that orgasms were the answer. I hadn't yet pulled off the trick of having one, but I knew that I wouldn't give up until I had. Yet how obvious was my fear that the energy which would be released if and when I *did* have one would blow away my whole safe world in a mushroom cloud of sexual fission? Indeed, before long the big-boy boyfriend was the first casualty of my new self-awareness.

I'm a dab hand at orgasms now. But, after the first one, I didn't really believe that I would be able to locate that feeble beacon of responsiveness again and amplify it into an orgasm for a second time. It had really been touch and go. The effort had been so enormous, the pay-off so brief, yet there had been enough of a buzz, my body had felt different enough to make me want to go to all the effort of trying again. It seemed important to repeat the exact same steps: that seemed the only guarantee of not getting lost down the dead-ends of my neuro-circuitry. Very quickly, though, that meant the whole thing became ritualised; I soon had an almost superstitious need to stick to exactly the same sequence, the same routine, otherwise nothing would happen. Bad idea, because it meant that the *knowledge* became arcane: how could anyone else possibly read the runes and follow the secret map to where O marked the spot? Surely no man could come anywhere near the mark, and it seemed pointless to try (*sooo* embarrassing too, all that 'up a bit, down a bit' and them expecting a *result* sharpish). Like Catherine Millet, I split off orgasms and sex. Sex was fun, a romp, a cuddle with knobs on; orgasms were private, sacred, pure sensation.

In many ways, an orgasm by your own hand is another sort of symbolic man, just like the crushes and long-distance lovers I've been collecting all my life. It's perfect self-love without the *inconvenience,* the demandingness, the unfathomable mystery of flesh in your bed. No attempt by a man to grope his way along the path to my orgasm has ever been successful and in fact the more actively they try to 'get it right', the less I like it. It isn't because they're bad at it (although maybe they are) but because I feel the pressure to respond mounting. My anxiety that they will be disappointed swamps the possibility of coming. I am faking it almost before we've begun. There doesn't seem any alternative. If I was completely honest – 'Ooh, ow, no, no thanks, it's not quite like that, no, no, it's okay, I'd rather do it myself, thanks' – the game would be up straight away. The faking seems inevitable. So although *I* can do the orgasm trick now, in a way it has alienated me even further from people I have sex with.

Chapter 16

MARK AS READ

A woman amuses her children hugely by telling them stories about her previous boyfriends. But both she and her husband know that soon she'll be making him the subject of a funny story.

Story idea, from a notebook, 2003 (age 41)

AROUND a year after I'd started seeing Christine I met the man whom I was eventually to marry. Because I didn't want him to think he was getting involved with someone who needed to see a therapist, I first of all kept my weekly sessions to myself and then, as he and I spent more time together, I became increasingly anxious to quit. Reluctantly, Christine let me stop, although she felt there was still work to do. The period of my life which is still my present began. I got married to a man with whom I had a great deal in common and with whom I felt at ease. I had children. But my pattern of dwindling commitment was still locked firmly in place.

Every enthusiasm I throw myself into seems to have a natural life of around two years – every hobby, every project, every relationship. This is distressing, making me seem like a flitting airhead. I have found some comfort in recent research which reported that at the beginning of a new relationship the brain releases increased amounts of neutrophins (which stimulate nerve growth, needed to plough new neural pathways through the brain to record all the new experiences you're having). The neutrophins are associated with the sensation of being truly, madly, deeply in love. But within two years the neutrophins decrease markedly, usually to be replaced by 'the cuddle hormone', oxytocin. It's at that stage that a couple will 'settle down', happy to watch television on the sofa together rather than tearing each other's clothes off. Oxytocin plays a part in many aspects of human interaction, including the bonding between a mother and child, the suppression of fear and the fostering of trust (as well as aiding childbirth and lactation). It is also released during both male and female orgasm. I began to wonder whether I might be deficient in this chemical purveyor of comfort? Not enough orgasms, not enough oxytocin.

Children are strong glue and so are one's home, one's routines, one's 'normality'. These constants hold everything together – or at least they can slow down the appearance of the cracks. I've been married for much longer than two years now, but just around that two-year high-tide mark I ceased to think I was the happiest I could be. After that point, very very slowly, things began to creep into my head – thoughts, fantasies, alternatives. I began to feel a desire to go back into my past to see whether any of the paths I *hadn't* followed might have led to greater happiness than the version I *had*.

When I added my name to the list of my school contemporaries on the Friends Reunited website, I hardly recognised any of their names. There was one girl I knew – Karen Holmes. She had been a member of the Belle Tones, before she became one of the victims of the group's cattiness (by the end there were more girls who'd been forced out than were still morbidly singing Carpenters' numbers in assembly), but I was still on Christmas-card terms with Karen so I wasn't going to contact her as a long-lost friend through Friends Reunited. Once a year was enough to hear about the pleasure she now took in bird-watching and silk-painting. I wondered whether there was any point sowing my name into such infertile ground. The fact that I have barely kept in touch with my friends from school and college is all part of that inability to stick with anything for the long haul. Sad.

I logged onto Friends Reunited again a couple of times. Each time a few new names had been added but the ones that meant nothing to me continued to predominate. Sometimes I would read the messages people had left about themselves. I read them out of curiosity but they were usually disappointingly bland, along the lines of: 'I've been married to Fliss (Nookie to her schoolfriends) for fourteen great years now, and we have three gorgeous daughters and a golden lab, Sukie. I'm a partner at Scissors, Paper & Stone management consultancy in Reading, with holidays in Vail or at our little cottage in Rye'. I would wonder how such ordinary-seeming kids came to be swept up in the great Thatcherite tide of managerial success and to land on these shores of boring but self-congratulatory affluence.

Then, one cold January night, I went onto the site and saw the name which I had been hoping to find all along: *Mark Sykes*.

Mark's name had the little envelope symbol next to it meaning that he had left a message. Would beautiful Mark have turned into a management consultant with a horsy wife like all the rest of them? Hoping very much that he had not, I clicked my mouse on the message.

'Hi. Anyone out there remember me? I've been out of the country for ages now. The only name that rings a bell on this site is Carrie Jones. Hello??'

I felt a deep twang in my belly as I read my own name. He remembered me! *Only me!* MEEEEEEE! I existed in Mark Sykes' memory where everyone else had faded greyly away. Just the simple act of his naming me validated me and made me feel instantly, wonderfully alive. The actual meaning of his words, their unloaded simplicity, was trampled into the dirt as I elaborated Mark's message into a coded plea for immediate and fabulous liaison. I invested that 'Hello??' with more feeling, more glutinous yearning than the strangulated '*Hello?*' at the end of Lionel Richie's eponymous song (the one where the beautiful blind art student sculpts a hideous likeness of the schmaltzy singer after running her fingers inquiringly all over his quivering features).

Of course I would get in touch with him. It never occurred to me not to. I gave no thought to what the possible consequences might be, or whether it was *seemly* for a married woman to be contacting an old boyfriend over the Internet. In that moment I was pure ego, wholly focused on myself and how I might feed myself more of the delicious nectar which the mere mention of my name in Mark Sykes' message had dripped into my body. I already had to have more.

Over two decades on, the Internet now offered me an irresistible chance to loop back across the years, to go back and cancel out the mistakes I'd made, or at least to try and explain them. The day of my seventeenth birthday, when I'd ridden my bike out into the countryside to try to avoid Mark's birthday visit, was a vivid memory still. No, more highly coloured than a memory, it had become one of my *core stories*, part of my personal mythology, told and retold until it had taken on a filmic quality: the ride up the long, summery hill, the hours hiding out in the field, my return, the wilted rose. Almost everything else about my brief and tentative relationship with Mark Sykes had faded away, but that afternoon remained, as did the tantalising clip of myself and Mark in my bedroom, just before my mother came home from work and scraped the needle across the soundtrack of our heavy petting session.

I pressed the Reply button on my screen.

'Dear Mark ,
I have to confess to feeling something of a lurch in my stomach when I read your message on the Friends Reunited website and saw my name…'

I had to be careful what I said. It was no good describing the intensity of my reaction too exactly, but on the other hand I didn't want him to think I had been unmoved. It had to seem within the bounds of normality – *nonchalant* – and yet it had to be suggestive, subtly suggestive, with just enough of a hint of my continued interest in him to enable him to pick up on it, if he wanted to, but also to ignore it, if he wanted to, without there being any kind of obvious rebuff. I gave Mark a brief account of my life since school but instead of making it sound as though I had been reasonably happy and successful on the paths I'd followed, I implied a feeble choice of career, enthusiasms allowed to wither, cowardly failures to take risks, all with a background hum of regretfulness – Edith Piaf I was not. Surely he would understand that underpinning all my regrets was my wilful throwing away of *him*?

The Net is a very potent means of communication. Its combination of immediacy and safety (in the sense that you are both reachable and, ultimately, unreachable) is highly seductive. No one sees you, if you don't want them to, no one needs know exactly where you are, no one hears your voice – there isn't even any handwriting to scrutinise: you can shape a persona for yourself, disguise your flaws, enhance your image, flirt with or insult someone and then, if you choose, simply block any comeback. Your messages fly instantaneously into the headspace of your correspondent, whilst the nature of the medium seems to discourage careful re-reading and re-drafting of what you write – you tap out your communiqué and, irrevocably, loose off your electronic arrow; it rarely fails to hit the bullseye. Then you wait for the reply. Anticipation of a new message in your inbox becomes one of the sweetest emotions you feel.

A day later Mark replied. He said it was great to hear from me and filled in a few more details of his present life, not much more than that. It was odd talking to someone so far away, both in time and place – he now lived in Germany – and yet having his words come so intimately and privately to me. It was also very strange – and enticing – to suddenly have privileged access to a man who, in truth, I barely knew, without having had to go through the process of looking to meet someone, choosing someone to try to get to know, and then cautiously revealing my interest in them. It's *those* steps which most smack of treachery when you're married: the looking.

What was the adult Mark like? He was appealingly laddish, and he was single. He didn't seem to have accumulated all the trappings of early middle age – he was still living the life of a young man. I liked that. I envied him his freedom. He still loved rock music, he still read books, and he had the laidback coolness of someone who has managed to evolve a life they actually enjoy. Every so often I said to myself, 'That's the *same* person, the *same* person who stood on the doorstep and rang your doorbell, the person who you took up to your bedroom – there *is* a real connection between you, you *do* know him,' but all that connection was really good for was skipping the preliminaries. It was such fun, jumping in.

The next time I mailed him I said that I didn't want to 'stray into the inappropriate' but that there was stuff from the past I would like to go into with him. I wanted to lure him in closer, but I also wanted him to have the chance to get out now, if he chose to. If he wanted something 'safe' to talk about, I added, what music was he into now?

Back came the reply, not instantly, but a couple of days later: *'Fuck safe'*. He confessed that he could barely remember anything about our long-ago relationship, if it could be called that, but he was interested to know what I remembered about it. Mark's not remembering gave me a degree of control: I could recreate the key scenes, I could put a gloss on them if I wanted to. I didn't intend to lie, but the idea of intensifying the memory of our teen passion had a definite appeal. I felt that I could somehow seduce the Mark Sykes of now with a Kodachrome reconstruction of our brief past together.

To begin with I was reticent about what I coyly referred to as the 'Bedroom Incident'. It was the only thing that had happened between us that was overtly sexual. I mailed Mark: *do you remember going up to my room after school? I'll tell you what I remember if you ask me to, but otherwise I won't.* I was still feeling my way. I didn't know whether this new Mark, Mark nearly a quarter of a century on, would enjoy hearing about his adolescent fumblings. *Yes*, he said, *tell me.* He *knew* he was consenting to my *writing* our past; it was part of our fledgling flirtation – more of a fantasy than a witness statement.

Like the day of my seventeenth birthday, the 'Bedroom Incident' had become mythic, glossily sexualised in my memory. It was no longer just an awkward groping session culminating in embarrassing near-discovery by my mum. We were a young Cybill Shepherd and Jeff Bridges in *The Last Picture Show*. The curtains at my bedroom window filtered the sultry sunlight and cast edible shadows over our skin. Our kisses were hungry. We were innocent and yet knowing, holding our breath at how far we were going even as slow sinful smiles spread over our faces. That moment when I heard my mother coming home brought it to an end, but it was also the supreme moment of our transgression, galvanising us with adrenalin, like a paparazzo's flashbulb going off.

Now I had the memory of that afternoon, that miserly quarter-portion of an afternoon, and in my imagination it stood for wonderful, swoony, naughty-innocent teenage sex, the sort of sex that I longed to have again, however ludicrous that might be in my forty-year-old married reality. Spinning out from that key fantasy came spools of luscious scenarios, all sunlit and drizzled with laughter: sex in flower-filled meadows, sex in the park, sex in the hay, sex in the dunes. The 'Bedroom Incident' shaped my expectations of sex for the rest of my life. But it had been cut short, never brought to a conclusion, and that too in its way had informed my life. I wanted *so badly* to go back and have that moment *again,* to have it properly, completely, happily. Would Mark be able to understand the power of my memories of him? Now that I was in touch with him again it was hard to resist the intense drive to reach back, to go back, to have now what I had once only nearly had.

The idea of 're-enacting' the B.I. (as we now referred to it) soon occurred to both of us. We had unfinished business, didn't we, and the idea of being together again, perhaps even in that same room, to complete something which had been interrupted more than twenty years earlier was a gorgeously transgressive fantasy and the first time that anything sexual was actually mooted between us.

I also told Mark, rather guardedly, that there was something I wanted to apologise for. What could that possibly be, he wrote back, he couldn't think of anything (well, his memory of the whole thing *was* virtually wiped clean). So I told him the story of running away from him on my birthday and the awfulness of coming back to the wilted rose and the line of empty teacups; and how very much I regretted what I'd done as it had brought things to an end between us. I think the sincerity of my apology probably left him rather nonplussed. But I did have a sense of having atoned for my past cruelty. Now I could get on with the business at hand.

How much fun is it possible to wring from a daily email to someone six hundred miles away? Enough fun to make me feel that I had retraced my steps in the sexual maze and found a completely new path to follow – an upfront, fearless, sexy new me was now striding confidently along this road to perdition. The best thing about it was that nothing ever seemed to overstep the mark. I might send an email full of questions about anything, anything I was curious about, and back would come the answers, with more questions that probed me even more intimately.

(Me to him: *'How many people have you slept with? Have you got any piercings? Tattoos? Have you read The Story of O?'* Him to me, rather shockingly: *'What's your favourite position? Do you masturbate? Do you normally come during sex?'* Hmm, tricky). I might tremble at the frankness of my retelling of some story from my past and wish that I hadn't sent it, but he always liked such things. A lot of our mails consisted of stories about ourselves and these stories created a sense of the confessional, of being the privileged listener, which I really loved.

True, we sounded intermittent notes of caution. We both

knew that if we ever met up, we might find that we did not compare to the shadow puppets of ourselves who twirled and danced for each other on the Net. Mark was particularly sensible about this, rather dishearteningly so. If I thought about it too much I reckoned he might not like the idea of an infatuated mother-of-two flinging herself at him with all the weight of her real, post-childbirth flesh – but I didn't think about it too much. In fact, it was me who pushed us closer towards the barrier where reality waited to collect us. It was me who chose to describe myself with not entirely necessary realism. It was me who took photos with my digital camera and emailed them to Mark without really being able to 'see' myself: having taken what I *thought* were pictures of myself in my best light – the results of a ludicrous session with the delayed shutter-release button on my camera – I looked at them and wondered whether in fact I actually looked really ugly. I just didn't know, but I sent them all the same. (The photograph that Mark sent me in return was maddening – he was just a tiny figure in the middle distance, but I pored over it. I just about convinced myself that I recognised something of the Mark Sykes I'd known in those few dots of colour, but really all I saw was a tall, pleasant-looking man with a friendly smile.)

It was scary to bring reality into our daily fictions but I had decided to drive things forward to the point where we could meet up and see what happened. So it was me who phoned Mark up on my mobile phone, sitting in the car one night feeling very nervous and guilty. Of course it was a let down. It was supposed to be thrilling but it was all rather mundane. And Mark's voice – it was not the voice I expected, not a voice from a film soundtrack, more like William Hague after a couple of pints. William Hague! Oh no!

'*You sound like William Hague!*' Could I have said anything more disconcerting? You sound like a balding Tory twit.

Me: What are you doing right now?
Him: Getting my supper, actually.
Me: Oh, have I called at a bad time?
Him: No, it's okay.
Me: Oh, good. So, how are you?
Him: Yeah, great. It's great to hear your voice.
Me: Yeah, you too.
Him: I don't really sound like fucking William Hague, do I?
Me: No, no, it's just you've got more of an accent than I thought you'd have.
Him: Oh.
Me: What are you doing tonight then?
Him: Nothing much, might read a book…

It was really difficult having a conversation with my computerised man, hard not to start whinnying with nervous laughter or seeking refuge in clumsy attempts at jokiness. The inrush of reality was hard to withstand, and I slightly regretted the new picture I now had of Mark, making himself a spot of supper and putting his feet up with a book. But soon we had hung up and I could retreat to my PC again and the comfort of words on a screen.

I rang Mark again a couple of times and it was less awkward, but talking on the phone really only served to point up the perversity of our supposed 'relationship'. The phonecalls parodied normal phone conversations – they were just supposed to be chats, moments of contact, but we didn't really have any small talk, no little tokens to exchange, because our frail friendship had no underpinning of flesh-and-blood normality. Once, though, after one of these calls, he sent me a text message: *'Your voice was seriously sexy there. Talk to me like that when we fuck.'* I kept that message stored on my phone for months and it was like a hip-flask of elixir. (I tried to text a reply to Mark's message but at the time I had never done texting and didn't know how to delete all the mistakes I made. Random sprinkles of punctuation kept appearing. Mark thought it was quite funny, but you could tell he didn't think it was very cool. I'm a nifty texter now.)

I still believed I could conjure up a real connection between us made only of words. I poured myself into my emails, they were concentrated Carrie juice. And to keep Mark sucking greedily at the bottle, I threw in some zestier ingredients. One night, I closed my eyes and, keeping my eyes tightly shut, I typed my fantasy of what it would be like if we met. How we would look into each other's faces to see if we recognised each other but then, whether we did or not, would allow ourselves to be overtaken by the erotic intensity of this chance coming together. It was hot, but it still wasn't real. And yet I felt more real than I had felt for a very long time. In 'real life' I had become completely invisible, passing through public places unnoticed, never admired, never desired. In the unreality of the Net, I could arouse desire, real blood pumping through real veins, just a few hundred miles away. And my own desire was more real than I had believed myself capable of feeling. I had that deep-belly throb which is completely involuntary and can't be called up at will – my body convulsed when I read the words *me fucking you*. And I had mouth-longing, a literal hunger for Mark's kisses; my mouth felt like a blooming flower, the petals ripening, a sexual organ. But, strangely, all this sexual intensity was locked up, beyond release. As I lay so still in bed, night after night, pretending to be asleep, I could surely have burned off some of that dangerous fuel with the friction of my own fingers, drawing on all that imaginary sex to hasten my own satisfaction? It just wouldn't happen. Perhaps I was 'saving myself' for Mark.

Throughout this period, the newspapers were full of articles about ex-lovers who had miraculously found one another again through the Friends Reunited website and who were now planning to marry their childhood sweethearts. The *Daily Mirror* ran a centre spread featuring photograph after photograph of plump women in sensible outfits, their arms hugging the slightly sagging waists of their reunited darlings, never to let them go again after their first carelessness. These were refound loves that could be celebrated openly, not potential marriage-wreckers. The stories about those came later, when Relate started to complain loudly that Friends Reunited was causing trouble in marriages, giving people false dreams of being able to go back in time and recapture their past. All these reports spoke directly to me: I envied those smug women in the *Mirror* who had not only found their lost boyfriends but managed to scoop them back up from wherever life had carried them. I couldn't accept that the dreams were always false. Some – *mine* – must surely sometimes come true?

The *Guardian* had a feature where a reader sent in an agony letter and other readers gave their advice. One of these letters was from a 53-year-old 'happily married' woman who was wondering whether to meet up with her first love after he had contacted her through Friends Reunited. I felt personally chided by the disapproval which almost all the published replies showed towards her. The woman described feeling as though she was in 'hormonal freefall', 'both excited and frightened by the intense feelings' she had been experiencing. *Yes, yes!* But lives would be devastated, warned the readers' letters, 'Are you insane?' 'Enjoy your memories of this man who is now probably fat, bald and unprepossessing'. 'Have a jolly afternoon talking over old times and then return to your wonderful husband'. It was all thoughtful, decent advice – they were *all* right, weren't they? But was there not a single *Guardian* reader who had felt moved to write in and say, if this old flame is lighting sparks in the dying embers of your sexuality, then for your own sake, find out what happens when you turn the heat up? That's how I was starting to justify what I was doing: I was saving myself from sexual death (not for the first time, I now see).

I had been feeling sour about sex, dismissive of its supposed pleasures. If there was sex on television I pulled a face and switched channels – why should anyone else have fun if I wasn't? I was in the process of creating a sexual politics wholly predicated on my own grim sex life: orgasms during intercourse were a myth; sex was just a selling tool for the advertising industry; everyone hated sex but wouldn't admit to it for fear of losing face... Now, suddenly, I discovered that my ability to respond sexually wasn't completely dead, as I had feared, but only dormant, and I was exultant. It was glorious to feel aroused, just by words on a screen, and it was this triumphant sense of resurrection that blocked out any guilt I felt about cheating on H, my husband, albeit in virtual reality. I saw myself as a ghost, a semi-transparent version of myself which could walk out of my flesh, leaving behind the husk of my dead self to carry on with the daily routine, cooking and eating meals, chatting about what was on telly, going frigidly to bed. Meanwhile the ghost girl stole off to write more sexy stuff, to send flirty text messages, to sink into the cloud of her daydreams.

If I was honest there was a slight pull between the Mark I created as the recipient of all that I wrote (the Mark who, in a sense, I *wrote*) and the Mark who came across in *his* words. How could there not be? He was himself, and his realness chafed a little against my imagination: he smoked, he went out drinking, he loved football, he was a regular 'guy'. But it wasn't long before I had rationalised all these things, and assimilated them into my image of Mark as the world's sexiest man – his very straightforwardness, his frank maleness, became the things which were most attractive about him. After all, Mark was only the latest in a long long line of unreal lovers. As for his telling me, more than once, that he was hoping to meet the right person, I thought maybe, somehow, that person might be me.

I decided I had to go and see him.

I had been letting things deteriorate with H by not stepping in to save us from miserable situations and corrosive moods. I hugged my secret new sexual aliveness to myself. I was losing weight magically, I was brighter eyed; I hopped about to pop music; the shops were suddenly full of great clothes. But no benefit came to my husband from this upswing. There came a point where we had to discuss our grim stand-off; of all days we chose to have the 'terrible talk' on Valentine's Day. He had not given me a card, and I had held back the one I had rather hollowly bought for him. The absence of the cards hung very heavily in the air and finally H said we would 'have to talk'. Those dreaded words! We sat at the empty kitchen table, food forgotten. Even as we talked painfully about the lost momentum of our marriage I felt detached from the seriousness of what we were saying to each other because I had the secret of Mark Sykes to hold close. The more I thought about it, the more acceptable it seemed that I should be allowed to find sexual happiness with someone else now that my feelings for H had fallen away. It was starting to feel like my right.

Carrie Jones

At around midnight I found myself telling H about Mark, playing down the sexual side of our renewed friendship, but saying that I wanted to go and see him, for old times' sake.

At first it seemed that, miraculously, everything was going to proceed according to my script. It was as if the engines of a plane we were on had failed in mid-air, but for a little while the aircraft was flying serenely on. My admission could not be unsaid now, but nothing cataclysmic had happened as a result. While the plane glided quietly towards oblivion, I booked a flight to Germany for the Easter weekend (still two long months away). After a couple of days, though, H started to react. He logged onto my computer while I was out, desperately trying to find out about my 'Internet lover'. Having discovered a name, he tried to track Mark down via the German electoral roll. Incredibly, he found a *different* Mark Sykes living in Germany and rang him up, leaving a spurious message and asking him to call our number at home. That night we had another painful talk and H told me what he had done. My anguish at the thought of H reading my emails, perhaps being able to resurrect deleted files, *seeing everything*, was intense. His rifling through my electronic handbag was probably justified in the light of *my* behaviour, or at least to be expected. And the feeling that my head had been violated was perhaps nothing in comparison to what H felt at *my* betrayal of him. But that night I went to sleep muttering black words of hatred under my breath.

The next day the Other Mark Sykes rang our house, asking for the pseudonym my husband had used in his message. I had answered the phone (H was at work). When the Other Mark Sykes said his name, I thought for a moment that it was *my* Mark, although he didn't sound right (no hint of William Hague about *this* Mark Sykes!) and he wasn't making sense. Who the hell was he asking to speak to? I said, 'It's *me*, Carrie,' then I suddenly worked out what was going on and had to bluster my way out of the situation, apologising for some vague mix-up having taken place.

H had taken what I thought of as my *personal* drama (which in my mind was all about *my* sexual responsiveness) and selfishly turned it into *his* drama, which was all about being betrayed. Of course, it was about that too, but so far I had managed not to think about it in those terms. The way *I* saw it, I was on a quest for sexual happiness, which had nothing to do with my marriage. My internet affair generated the same levels of self-absorption as masturbation, and I certainly didn't share that with H. Alone in front of my screen, I set the whole of my life – husband, kids, home – aside: all that mattered was the hope of one short daily email, whose few drops of sweetness I would try to savour long after I had sucked them dry. But weren't those emails getting a little shorter, a little less sweet, as the weeks went on? Easter still seemed a very long way away.

I was desperate to maintain my sense of connection to Mark until we met up. Deprived of the warmth of real sunlight and the oxygen of actual contact, our poor, etiolated relationship was becoming spindly. I felt that, to keep it alive, I had to increase the intensity of the limited sensations available to us: *more* fantasies (or rather, my urgently imagined ideas of what reality might be like for us), *more* photos (just very slightly more revealing than the first lot). I wanted to 'talk' to him online in real time, and we both downloaded instant messaging software so that we could do that.

Then Mark emailed me to tell me he had met a girl and was starting a relationship with her. Our planned weekend together could only go ahead on the understanding that it would be platonic. The flirty emails, the text messages, the secret phonecalls all had to stop. I didn't feel angry. I understood. He was doing the decent thing by his new girlfriend, doing what I would have wanted him to do for me in the same circumstances: tying up his sexual loose ends. And the words he used to tell me were sincere. Mark had always been more realistic about the whole thing than me – *he* had never made the mistake of thinking that the brief and intermittent flickering of words across six hundred miles constituted a relationship. And he had said to me several times that he wanted to meet someone special, he wanted to be in a proper relationship. Why on earth would he turn down that possibility because of the ghost-worship of a frustrated housewife and mother on the other side of the continent?

I tried to hide my heartache but, after a couple of hours, tears began to ooze out of my eyes. I couldn't stop them, however strong I tried to be. I ended up being comforted, heroically, by H as I cried and cried. What husband should have to do that? I had told him the story of Mark Sykes, The Early Years, and he understood the pull of that golden-age memory. Maybe, as he held me, he felt a sense of reprieve, or relief, that I had been let go by a man he saw an aggressor, out to take me and destroy our family. Perhaps he saw Mark's disappearance as a chance to get me back. Me, I had to bury my feelings for Mark Sykes once more.

Something strange happened to my relationship with H. Our marriage was violently convulsed by my so-called affair with Mark, and, for a while, my 'carrying on' even seemed to have injected it with vital energy. Where before we had been wary of each other and increasingly withdrawn, now there was gallows humour and a cautious willingness to reveal something of our real sexual feelings. We had some frank conversations which I found I enjoyed; even though it felt dangerous to open up, the sky didn't fall in on us and we felt a little closer. For a long time I had been existing in a state of heated arousal and it was a sort of relief to redirect some of those feelings towards H. It could have been a temptation to imagine H was Mark, but I didn't do this, except once when H came home from a work party reeking of cigarette smoke and, instead of hating it, I buried my face in his clothes and thought of Mark. But, as time went on, it became clear that this was an interlude rather than a permanent change. The old coldness returned. I feel that I have split in two, or that a pre-existing split has now been formalised: there is stiff, unresponsive, 'frigid' Married Carrie, and dirty, aroused Secret Carrie. It's hard to imagine how I could integrate the two.

When the day on which I would have been flying to see Mark finally came around, long after I had stopped looking for his name in the list of the day's fresh emails, it so happened that I was going down to London to be in the audience for an early morning TV show – I think I was deliberately looking for things to do to buck myself up. I had to leave the house at four o'clock in the morning, in dense fog, and drive myself down through the near-deserted streets of East London. The only people I saw seemed dazed, standing on the pavements or walking across the road at wild angles: cleaning ladies and pop-eyed clubbers. I felt ethereal, not quite solid, the pressure of the silence in the car hissed in my ears, but the radio seemed unbearably intrusive. The last segment of the journey was across Hackney Marshes, as the sun was just starting to show above the horizon and the mist was burning off. Twists of vapour snaked above the ground as I floated over the deserted marsh, which was surreally beautiful.

It was a bad idea to do this TV thing alone. I had no one to share the awfulness of it, no one to offset the weird alienation

I was starting to feel. We had been told to come to a car park in Bow and wait to be transferred to the studio by coach. This car park was in the most derelict part of London. Burnt out cars blocked the pavements and smashed glass formed a thick mosaic on the ground. The car park itself was a vandal's world of adventure, the deep potholes turning the last few metres of my journey into a fright ride. It was touch and go whether I actually got out of the car or simply turned around and fled, but I wanted to earn the bad-taste brownie points that would come from attending this kitsch-fest.

So, at half-past five in the morning, I stood alone in a large, cold, bored crowd and watched the first of the day's planes taking off from City Airport nearby and flying across the red disc of the rising sun. It was from City Airport that my flight to Germany, to Mark, was to have departed. No coaches came to take us to the studio. A girl with a clipboard and defiantly bare grey arms came and yelled at us to form a line so that we could be frogmarched through the badlands to the studio. At the exact time that my flight would have been due, I watched a plane rising up in front of the new day's sun and tried not to cry.

Chapter 17

ALL THE THINGS I'M SCARED OF

> *Title Ideas:*
> *Peepshow*
> *The Wrong Bicycle*
> *The Trials of My Desire*
> *What I Wanted and What I Got*
> *E-Stranged*
> *The Girl Who Read O*
> *Cutting Up Playgirl*
>
> **From a notebook, 2006 (age 43)**

YESTERDAY evening I was standing looking out of my bedroom window at a car that was parked on the opposite side of the road. A woman was sitting inside and something about her, even at that distance, communicated her state of arousal, like a cloud of midges round her head. She was over-alert, fizzing. As I watched, another car drew up on our side of the road, a metallic blue sports car. She wound down her window, said something to the driver of the sports car, then both cars drove off in opposite directions. Seconds later, the blue car had turned round and came roaring down the hill to follow the woman. I felt excited to have secretly watched this encounter, even though I knew nothing about what was going on. To me it seemed obvious that it was an illicit, sex-driven meeting, and even if it wasn't, that's how I chose to interpret it.

What would have happened if I had had *my* version of that

rendezvous? If I had flown to Germany and come face to face with Mark Sykes in the sterile arrivals lounge of a German airport? What would that moment have been like? When all my efforts to create a sense of reality through words were actually transformed into *real* reality? Of course I had imagined our meeting over and over again – the smiles, the awkwardness, the holding of his gaze, the kiss on the cheek that would hold the promise of kisses to come. Or maybe it would have been something a bit more businesslike to cover up our confusion – the carrying of bags, the smart walk to the train platform, and then, on the firm banquette of the train, perhaps a first touch. Yes, but what if he looked at me and saw a tired girl, strung out on the hope of rescue, and knew straight away that he didn't want to be my rescuer? What if his flesh just said, nope, no thanks, sorry. What if *mine* did (a scenario I was only just able to make myself include in the set of possibilities)? In our emails, we had always paid lip service to the possibility that things 'wouldn't work out', but I had been willing to go a long way to find out whether they would.

And let's say we had been able to transmute fantasy into reality, and the famous 'dirty weekend' had come to be. By Monday lunchtime I would have been back on a plane to London, heading back to happiness, family-style. For how long would that have been tolerable? What guilt would have seeped into me? What resentment at the briefness of the freedom I had tasted? It doesn't matter any more, because the door has been locked again and the fantasy of Mark Sykes is serving a life sentence in my head.

Yet I *have* undergone a lasting transformation. The sensations I experienced during my contact with Mark dug new grooves through my synapses. Now I need something else to run through them to keep me feeling alive. The drive to write this book has been fuelled by the urge to fill the void left by the end of the affair that never was. What I'm left with, otherwise, is the life I had before. When the first email from Mark arrived, that life became a background, sometimes annoyingly distracting, sometimes dreamily faint, but when our brief electronic liaison ended, back it came, more starkly illuminated than before, the flaws in it all the more apparent. I haven't even been able to hold on to the feelings I felt thanks to Mark; it seems the body doesn't have a memory. The addictively sweet cocktail of endorphins and hormones has been flushed out and I can't call up those sensations again just by the power of thought.

It is possible for one's sexual side to grow pale and perhaps even die, or at least to become atrophied and then comatose. I can see that happening to me. I'm as conflicted as I've ever been about what I can and should do. The same warring factions – the puritanical sufferer who doesn't want to upset anyone and the self-indulgent chancer who can't say no – are still locked in an unedifying struggle with no foreseeable outcome. Recently I've started having fleeting visions of catastrophe: I imagine my car smashing into the crash barriers on the motorway, see myself falling into stairwells, or 'losing it' and just running away. A cataclysm, some sort of 'bomb' going off in my life over which I would have no control and for which I therefore couldn't be held responsible, is enormously attractive to me since I can't sensibly reconcile the contradictory parts of my personality. Nor can I face the pain I would cause if I changed my situation to one that selfishly suited me better.

In this stagnant fixity, the zombie wife-and-mother plods on while poor old Dirty Carrie is left with not much more than her guilty little sessions surfing the Net, looking at pictures. My terror of being eaten alive by credit-card scamsters means I never actually sign up for anything, but merely peep in through the windows one can find in the form of free clips and images.

My struggle to keep myself alive sexually with digital imagery has merely intensified my awareness that I am deprived of the real thing. Unlike written erotica, visual porn leaves nothing to the imagination; seeing real people actually performing your secret fantasies has the effect of devaluing them. The acts are somehow normalised by being enacted, their power as fantasies fatally undermined. And the people acting them out are almost never the people you would choose for your real-life experiences.

So porn doesn't really do it for Dirty Carrie any more – she never seems to find the perfect image to match what's in her head. It's hard to square my secret sexual self with my sterile 'real-time' role. Yet I seem unable to integrate sexual pleasure into my life. The story of my experience seems to be that sex is 'dirty' and the pleasure to be had from it always transgressive. The excitement about sex that hid away as a child has never properly re-emerged to take its rightful place in my adult life. This means I have to leave my 'proper' life and go somewhere else for pleasure – the Internet, a book, a secret affair...

I had always wondered whether a vibrator would be the answer to my prayers, but I had (of course) always been too shy to find out. But as my desire for sexual satisfaction waxed and waned, I came closer to daring to get one. At college, during that strange period of sexual madness, I found the courage to send off for a sex catalogue from the small ads in the back of the *Sun,* the clincher being that it promised a free vibrator with every copy. It didn't occur to me that the flat brown package that arrived in my pigeon hole was The Thing, the dangerously explosive device which I had so daringly sent off for. Having picked up my post on the way to lunch, I opened it while standing in the queue for the refectory. A cream-coloured finger pointed at me. Of course I had to go and hide it straight away, and I don't think I ever got over the shock of seeing that off-white wand which looked so like the 'Home Doctor' a friend and I had once found in the bottom of her mother's wardrobe and been horrified by. I just didn't like the look of the thing and I never believed that it would do anything for me, so naturally it didn't. If I had trusted it, the buzz might have hurried along my first orgasm by around fifteen years, but instead it became a kind of horror-film golem, screaming to be found wherever I hid it. In the end, I had to bring about a Mafia-type end to its hold over me: one morning I threw it into the foundations of a house that was being built on the route I took on my bike each day to the Faculty of Modern Languages.

No more vibrators for me, after that, even though I often thought longingly about replacing alienated boyfriends with something I could deal with more straightforwardly. Even when the Internet let me browse the shelves of virtual sex shops incognito, I was still too paranoid about discovery to get myself tooled up. I only had to imagine the excited cries of the children as they insisted on helping mummy open her parcel, or the pale shame of a husband who finds he has been cuckolded by the silicon intruder in his wife's knicker drawer.

Then, one Saturday, I went to White Cube in Hoxton Square to see Gilbert and George's beautiful but sterile installation of blown-up sex ads. I wandered around for as long as I could (about five minutes), admiring the lovely shade of red and the lovely shade of orange they had used, then I grew bored and left. *But*, conveniently around the corner, was Sh!, the women-only sex shop which I had already scrutinised on the Internet. A quick check in my A-Z, and I walked down the right dingy street to find the shop. There it was, looking exactly like your standard *men*-only sex shop. I couldn't bring myself to go in. I walked past, trying not to look as though I was peering through the beaded curtain hanging in the open doorway, but peering all the same. I didn't fancy feeling those beads brushing my face as I went in.

Then, when I had reached the main road, I made myself turn around and go back. I told myself sternly that it was now or never. The whole point of a women-only sex shop was surely to provide a kindly environment for jittery girls like myself. There was money to be made bringing Os to the ordinary. The bottom line was, I wanted to know if a vibrator would provide a short-cut through the muscle-wearing work-out that was my routine route to orgasm. This was my chance. There was cash in my pocket. I swept back the chinking beads and ducked inside.

The first thing I saw was a *man*. Come *on*, this was breaking the rules before I'd even summoned up the courage to look at the goods. The shop was very small and he was enthusiastically examining a harness by which a person might be suspended in mid-air. He was with a woman, and it was impossible not to hear him saying to her, in the full, confident tones of the upper-middle class, 'Darling, this is just what we were after, isn't it? I'm sure it would take your weight.' Darling herself seemed a little more diffident and, I'm sure, resented the reference to her physicality – better, surely, for him to pretend that she was gossamer-light and unimpinged upon by gravity. But this was clearly an arena of frank reality. Next, I saw a mother and daughter examining vibrators together. The idea that I might do such a thing with *my* mother is so violently, emetically alien that I had trouble sharing the space with them. But at the same time I was fascinated. Who was helping who? Was the experienced senior sagely advising her child to learn about her body with the help of a sex aid? Or was the enlightened daughter gamely treating her mum to a bit of no-strings fun after the trauma of divorce? Horribly, it seemed that they were just out shopping together, blithely comparing girths and hefts as they might select a new pepper-grinder in John Lewis.

By now my failure to make eye contact with the merchandise was starting to become conspicuous. I was quite worried that I might get thrown out for not having the right attitude. Darling and her man were putting the harness on Mastercard now, and the mother and daughter had gone downstairs. On a side counter were dildos and vibrators in an untidy heap, obviously much tested and considered by hands determined to get just the right thing. Of course, there was a Rampant Rabbit, the best-selling vibrator, but, with its strange component parts (the bubblegum beads, the creepy 'thumb') it looked somehow as if it couldn't make up its mind what to be. The upfront flesh facsimiles were more my idea of what you would want – a simulacrum to take the place of an absent phallus. But my wanting one and my getting one were a short, thick pole apart. I just couldn't, *couldn't*, say (or infer) to another human being, however thick-skinned and profit-minded, 'I want this, please, to make up for the pleasure I'm missing out on in the normal run of things.' But I did want one. I had invested so much nerve in just getting inside the shop, it would be criminal to waste the opportunity now. My fingers barely making contact with them, I sorted gingerly through the range, affecting an intense interest in the price tags. And in fact they were fearfully expensive. I suppose you're paying the price for the orgasms, not the couple of pounds of prosthetic flesh. And who can put a price on pleasure? In the end, in a compromise for which I would quickly despise myself, I took from a display rack the tiniest vibrator money could buy, modelled to resemble nothing so much as a tampon. It was bubble-packed onto a cardboard backing, which meant I could hand it to the sales assistant face down. It could have been a new toothbrush. Lost in the folds of a gigantic carrier bag (plain, naturally), I carried the mini-machine out of the shop and home, where I hid it among my tampax, where I knew no one would ever look.

Was it worth it? Well, in spite of being tiny, it did work. But the hyperactive mosquito whine it made was horribly intrusive. And I felt the absence of a man, the space above me and inside me where there should be presence, too keenly to be wholly grateful for the spasm that tiny plastic plug induced.

Time went on and there was so much upfront talk of vibrators that I was emboldened. Maybe a nice big vibrator really would be a simple way to simple, uncomplicated pleasure. On a trip to Oxford Street I staked out the Ann Summers flagship store, newly refurbished to reflect their new, unsleazy image. I stood a knight's move away, across the road, watching how many people were going in and out. Hardly anyone, it seemed. Was that good or bad? Fewer people to see me, but fewer people behind whom to hide. I slipped off my wedding ring – this seemed important. Then I put my sunglasses on and crossed the road. Two dignified women were strolling out of the shop with carrier bags, not embarrassed, not ashamed. That could be me! The sunglasses were good, a spy's disguise, and I went up to the shop front. Instantly a greeter-girl zipped out to vacuum me in and I found myself standing just inside the door. *In!* Through the sultry gloom I could just make out joke books and chocolate willies, feather-trimmed nighties and PVC skirts. Deep black shadows hinted at inner sanctums. Very reluctantly I had to take the sunglasses off, in spite of the sanctuary they offered, as I knew I must look ludicrous. The darkness adjusted to glamour lowlight.

All the good stuff was downstairs. There's something about doing things you're scared to do. Once you've begun, the thing unfolds; you're still scared, but it's happening in spite of you. You can't believe you're walking down the stairs, walking towards the table with dozens of vibrators on it, looking at them, but you are. You can't believe that a cute little Scandinavian girl in plaits is smiling at you and asking you if you know which one you want, but she is. And when you shake your head, she starts to tell you which ones she personally *loves*, although this is the one she is *saving up* for, and now she is pressing the purple thing into the side of your nose and saying, *'Feel that!'* I am in a sex shop with a girl testing out a vibrator on my face. I am still alive. She is nice. I buy the purple thing. The carrier bag is nice. I leave the shop, dignified.

That I was able to do this meant a lot to me. I was genuinely scared to do it (weird though that may seem), but I did it, and afterwards I felt very pleased with myself, although a little foolish – turned out it wasn't *quite* the death-inviting parachute jump I'd imagined. I want to do all the things I'm scared of.

Very recently I went to an afternoon screening of a foreign film. It was being shown in one of those tiny rooms in a Leicester Square multiplex where the screen is not much bigger than a luxury TV. I arrived just before the film was going to start and the cinema was already in darkness. By the light of the trailer that was playing, I saw that there was only one other person there: the dome of a male head was just visible above a head-rest. I stood in the aisle. I was afraid to sit in the dark with a strange man who might pester me, or worse. I turned to go and ask if a member of the cinema staff could sit in on the screening. But as I opened the door to go out, someone else was coming in, another man.

'Oh, good, are you coming in? Because I was just feeling a bit nervous...' I was babbling. The man looked at me very briefly and went and sat down. I sat down too, the three of us making an almost perfect equilateral triangle as far apart as we could be in that small space. The film started and I began to be engaged by it, but at the same time I found myself fantasising about the second man: what if he came over and sat next to me? What if we started kissing in the darkness? What if we found ourselves leaving together? And we *did* find ourselves leaving together. He walked down the stairs behind me, I could hear his footsteps in rhythm with my own, my heart started to race. Then, abruptly, they stopped. I glanced behind me and saw the door of the men's lavatory swinging shut. So, no fantasy sex about to happen there. One stranger, then, is a rapist, another a seducer. What makes the difference?

The trouble is that I find it so hard to forget the feeling that I used to get when a man became my lover. That feeling of being *chosen* is the purest boost to one's self-esteem that I know. Once married, the need for such validation is supposed to cease, but I don't think it does. For me, the sense of being special died away, just as it had with my boyfriends (the two-year thing) but now I was caught in marriage's net, bound up with responsibilities to children. My interest in sex with the person I was supposed to be closest to died away, because in my head I was making myself available for the *next* wonderful man, the one who was going to come and make me feel wonderful again. I could leave, as thousands do every year, but for now I don't, partly because of the desolation it would wreak on the others involved and partly because I fear the structurelessness and poverty that might await me and my children.

I've become addicted to agony columns, not for the usual snicker of laughter at other people's stupidity, but because I identify so strongly with those who write letters begging to be told that they have not done wrong: the sex they had with their best mate's boyfriend was 'mind-blowing', they 'can't stop thinking about' their boss, their teacher, their stepfather. Surely, they seem to plead, the unleashing of passion in a dull life is justification enough, just tell me it's okay. But, with one voice, the *agonistas* doggedly wheel out their kindly condemnations – don't do it, no good will come of it, go back and work on your marriage, always that, *work at it*, you can make it come right, just learn to relax, learn to communicate, learn to resuscitate the dead. I'm reading their replies less and less now; I just want to hear about the *crimes*.

There seems to be a fad in newspapers and magazines for articles about loss of sexual desire in women. 'Female sexual arousal disorder' is the new bulimia and there are countless reassuring items offering advice on how to 'bring back that loving feeling'. I expect editors think they are bravely tackling one of the last taboo subjects – frigid women – but all the emphasis seems to be on *treatments*. Swallow this and you'll soon be chemically 'gagging for it' again: Viagra, phentolamine, bromocriptine, testosterone or, if these drugs sound scary, try vitamin B5, ginseng, or wild Mexican yam. But the assumption always seems to be that, if only you could get your body working properly, you'd be delighted to resume a sprightly sex life with your lovely husband who is patiently waiting for everything to 'come right again'. No one ever seems to come out and say, well, maybe you just don't want to sleep with him any more.

How much easier my life would be, though, if I *could* take a pill or rub on a cream which made the prospect of marital sex agreeable. I would happily take something to be freed from the guilt of wishing I was somewhere else, to stop feeling like a blow-up doll.

When I thought I was going to go and see Mark, I started taking the Pill again after a long long break. Six months passed and it was time to renew the prescription. I'm a great collector of newspaper articles (it's in my genes: when we used to go and visit my granny every Saturday, as we went in through the front door she would always appear from her back kitchen brandishing a handful of cuttings from the *People's Friend* and the *Daily Express* about pills and ointments and therapies which we would have to listen to while we ate our pork pies. We always had pork pies). Only a few days after I had begun taking the first packet of pills, a fat headline had appeared in the *Daily Mirror*: KILLER PILL. It named the very brand that I'd been prescribed as increasing the risk of lethal blood clots. It felt like the icy hand of retribution tightening around the back of my neck. By the time I had taken all six packets, I was still alive but I was wary about taking more of the stuff, especially when I was practically celibate. So as soon as I sat down in my doctor's room, I took out the *Mirror* cutting, yellowing now, and a page torn from the *Sunday Times* Style section detailing all the things you can be prescribed for loss of libido.

The doctor blinks at them. How they must hate the cuttings addicts, the self-diagnosers with their print-outs from Internet health sites. He's young, Doctor T, with startled eyes and moist lips, but he took us on when we moved to this town, in spite of the practice's lists being full, and he seems kind.

I've had to take the kids to the appointment with me and they immediately throw themselves down on the floor to look at the car-boot-sale books and toys provided for them.

'I'm running out of pills, but, what with all this stuff in the paper [I shake the *Mirror* cutting], I don't know if it's worth taking it any more.' I look down at the tops of the children's heads and mouth, 'I don't really need it… Maybe you could help me with some of this stuff?' (shaking the *Sunday Times* page now).

He barely glances at the dense page of type, so many remedies crammed into one page. Does he have a slight squint or is he just focusing on me from too short a distance?

'Is everything alright at home? How do you feel about making love? he asks me sweetly.

Just this degree of mild concern has me blinking back tears even while it is making me shrivel with embarrassment. My oldest child looks up at me and tries to tune in to the whispered talk.

'I just can't do it. I feel a sort of revulsion. But I know I *can* get turned on because I felt like that about someone else a while ago…'

Doctor T is all damp concern. I'm grateful for his not dismissing me as a silly neurotic woman, but I'm panicking at the depths he seems to want to plumb with barely any preamble. I suppose you can still only have your ten-minute appointment, even if you need full-blown psychotherapy.

'Do you love your husband?'

'I… I… well, I suppose so…' *I can't answer that!* Especially not with the children there.

'What are you talking about, Mummy?'

Ignoring my child, I feebly wag the cutting with the nice, easy answers on it: *Ask your doctor for a blood test and a referral to a sexual function clinic.* 'So you don't think any of this would…?'

He smiles; it's a shame he looks like a nervous choirboy. 'When ladies go off making love, it's usually down to problems with the relationship. You need to think about what *you* want. Be selfish. Maybe you need to go and live on a desert island. You've got to do what *you* really want to do.'

No more Pill then? He shakes his head. 'It doesn't seem there's much point, does it?'

He hands me a tissue as the tears finally start to fall and pats my hand. 'Be selfish. Be *selfish*.'

I gather together coats and jumpers and bags and children and struggle out of the room.

By writing this book, I have been selfish. I have enjoyed writing up all my stories and sieving them out from the slurry of regret. My sexual autobiography has turned out to be the story of a divided self, a kind of 'Frigid Jones's Diary'. In giving expression to the conflicts within my sexuality, to the desires I've hidden and the 'frigidity' that has so often afflicted me, I feel I'm maybe staking out some ground which other women will now come and claim as common to them too. Our secret notebooks may be filled with the names of millions of different people, but all of us have a notion of what we wanted, and all of us are waking up each morning to what we got.

Most of all, I want my book to be a counter-balance to all the phoney stuff about girls and women that so often gets promoted as 'the truth', all the trite rubbish that is sold under the banner of 'chick-lit'. I hate the way that clichés about sex and love are repeated and repeated until they seal over the separateness and difference that is each of us. If I have had to come out and admit that, well, it wasn't *quite* the way it was supposed to be for *me* – I wore the big pants but I didn't get the guy – I don't mind, as long as somebody somewhere thinks that my version is more interesting, or funnier, or just more *real*.

I started writing this book in response to the ending of something – the end of my fantasy about Mark. In some way, it surely also marks the end of my marriage, although, officially, that goes on. It feels as though that relationship has already had many endings, each one more definitive than the one before, like a corpse bouncing down a mountain. You think you've reached the bottom, some point of affectless rest, then a new rattle of falling debris sends you just that little bit lower, rendering you more contemptuous, more determined to get out, should an opportunity present itself. But it doesn't seem to.

Writing is an activity that colludes with you. It's absorbing, gratifying, and creates the powerful illusion of escape to another world, another existence. At the same time it's keeping you exactly where you are, wasting time, not really changing anything. But the alchemy of publication can sometimes achieve that. If this book gets out there, is read, liked, commented on with occasional kindness and a sense of recognition, I think that will change me. The book, then, will be a beginning, not an ending. Validated by it, as I have always longed to be – by a parent, a teacher, a lover – I will perhaps feel that I can change my life, in order to live it in a way that reconciles those cowering, secret aspects of my personality with my more concrete and, so far, frankly, dull existence. The only answer, in the end, is to live in the light, not hiding, and to accept that, whilst one might be rejected, vilified, by some, the light will also enable you to be found by other, likeminded souls.

Love may come, even to the weird.